Still Living, Still Learning

Meditations

on Moving

Beyond Loss

June Titus

kregel
PUBLICATIONS

Grand Rapids, MI 49501

Still Living, Still Learning: Meditations on Moving Beyond Loss

© 2000 by June Titus

Published by Kregel Publications, a division of Kregel, Inc., P.O. Box 2607, Grand Rapids, MI 49501. For more information about Kregel Publications, visit our web site: www.kregel.com

Unless otherwise indicated, Scripture quotations are from the *New King James Version.* © 1979, 1980, 1982, Thomas Nelson, Inc., Publishers.

Scripture quotations marked NASB are from the *New American Standard Bible®,* © The Lockman Foundation 1960, 1962, 1963, 1968, 1971, 1972, 1973, 1975, 1977. Used by permission. (www.Lockman.org)

ISBN 0-8254-3824-1

Printed in the United States of America

1 2 3 4 5 / 04 03 02 01 00

*In memory of my dear and loving husband, Jim,
and with gratefulness to Alma Griffin
who believed my book should be published
and saw that it reached this publisher.*

Preface

It has always been easier for me to write about my feelings than to express them verbally.

The feelings that followed the death of my husband were even harder to express aloud. True, I could share what I felt with other widows, and I appreciated their caring. I also appreciated the caring of those who could only hug me and say, "I'm sorry." I especially appreciated the caring of our children and family; they were sorrowing, too.

All the caring helped, but there were still lonely days, and especially nights, of sorrow such as I had never known before. I needed to face these myself, with my Savior and God.

Comfort and help came in quiet times alone, when I was praying and reading God's Word. It came in memories. One in particular stood out.

I remembered a day not too many months before my husband died. He had his arms around me, and I said, "I don't know what I would do without you." And although he held me tighter, he answered in his gentle, sensible way, "You'd go on living."

And I did! I have! Jim was right.

I began to wake up in the morning and say, "What do you have for me to do today, Lord?"

I found out that my days did not need to be filled with "important" tasks and activities. No, mostly it was little things that brought a smile to my face and made others smile, too. Or events that set me to thinking. Conversations shared or overheard. A beautiful scene—even an everyday one. They all led to special thoughts.

Inspirations came from everyday living!

Writing this devotional book has given me such joy that I wondered if perhaps God could use it to encourage others. That is my prayer.

*Blessed be God, even the Father of our Lord
Jesus Christ, the Father of mercies, and the God of all
comfort; who comforteth us in all our tribulation,
that we may be able to comfort them which are
in any trouble, by the comfort wherewith we
ourselves are comforted. (2 Cor. 1:3–4 KJV)*

Learning

"Take My yoke upon you and learn from Me,
for I am gentle and lowly in heart, and you will
find rest for your souls." (Matthew 11:29)

Learning: it begins at birth and continues throughout life. Some learning is easy; some is difficult. But living is learning. Although I've spent more than sixty years in learning, somehow, the realization that I still have much more to learn has fully dawned upon me in the last eight years. Perhaps it was the shock of widowhood. There is no way of knowing what it will teach you until you experience it. Of course, that is true of everything. As I begin a new phase of learning, my thoughts turn more and more to the importance of Jesus' words, "Learn of me." True wisdom and understanding come from Him.

As children we depend on our parents and those who are older to teach us; we are eager to learn when we are young. "I can do it myself" goes the familiar cry. Ah, yes!

The lessons become harder as we grow older. With the psalmist we cry, "So teach us to number our days, that we may gain a heart of wisdom" (Ps. 90:12).

God is patient and loving. He has a purpose in the lessons He teaches. All that He teaches is for our good. He has not promised that it would always be easy. But a yoke means that we are joined together with Him in the learning. That helps. And I keep learning.

Prayer

*Thank You for the lessons that You have taught me today,
Father. I'm glad that You don't mind repeating them.
Help me especially to learn to be content, loving, kind,
and thankful. In Jesus' name. Amen.*

Learning During Our Stay upon Earth

And if you address as Father the One who
impartially judges according to each man's work,
conduct yourselves in fear during the time of your stay
upon earth. (1 Peter 1:17 NASB)

My times are in Your hand. (Psalm 31:15)

Knowing my "stay upon earth" is in my Father's hands gives me peace and assurance. He has promised that if, "in all [my] ways [I] acknowledge Him . . . He shall direct [my] paths" (Prov. 3:6).

I was almost seventeen when I accepted Christ as my Savior and Lord. My parents had taken me to church ever since I was a small child. I sat quietly between my father and mother, scribbling in a little notebook my father gave me. I learned early I was to be quiet in church. I learned as I grew older to sing the hymns. I learned simple Scripture verses and easy prayers. But it was not until I truly understood that I was a sinner for whom Christ died that I learned of my need to accept Him personally as Savior. He has been teaching me ever since, and I keep learning.

I learned to be a wife, mother, and homemaker. Those were precious years. I learned to let go (that was a difficult lesson) as my sons became grown men and husbands. I learned to love my daughters-in-law. I found a new joy in learning to be a grandmother. Then, at fifty-seven, I learned to face the death of my mate of more than thirty-five years. I had faced the deaths of grandparents, a great-grandmother, and friends, but this death was part of me. It was a difficult lesson that drew me closer to my Lord. Now I am learning to be the daughter that elderly parents need.

Prayer

I pray, Lord, that You will use the experiences
and thoughts that I share in this book as a testimony
to Your faithfulness, wisdom, and sufficiency
for every need. In Jesus' name. Amen.

A New Lesson

Blessed be the God and Father of our
Lord Jesus Christ, the Father of mercies
and God of all comfort. (2 Corinthians 1:3)

"Why don't you write down your feelings?" suggested my sister.

The grief I felt after my husband's death seemed too much to bear at times. My sister's suggestion proved to be the therapy I needed.

I realized early on that although many people were grieving every day, *grief is extremely personal.* I deeply appreciated the cards, calls, and consolation from others. It helped to know they cared. But my greatest help was the same as had sustained and carried me through the difficult days of my husband's illness. I turned to God's Word and again was comforted by His precious promises.

For if we believe that Jesus died and rose again,
even so God will bring with Him those
who sleep in Jesus. (1 Thessalonians 4:14)

God had not left me without comfort. As always, I arose from time in His Word and prayer comforted with an inner strength that could only come from Him. I had none of my own. I knew others were praying for me, too. Their prayers were being answered.

I appreciated the strength God gave to others. My husband died in Alaska where we were visiting our second son and his wife. They, though grieving themselves, made arrangements for my trip home with our son accompanying me. Our precious daughter-in-law had administered CPR to my husband until the ambulance arrived. She now would see about the required autopsy. Our other two sons, my brother, and our oldest son's wife were at the airport when we arrived home. This daughter-in-law had a meal prepared. Family love surrounded me.

And underneath are the everlasting arms.
(Deuteronomy 33:27)

Prayer

Thank You for the comfort You provide through Your precious
Word and through prayer, Lord. In Jesus' name. Amen.

Learning in Times of Mourning

And Sarah died . . . in the land of Canaan;
and Abraham went in to mourn for Sarah and to
weep for her. (Genesis 23:2 NASB)

Jesus wept. (John 11:35)

Tears! They flow until you wonder that there are any more left. I have always cried easily and often felt ashamed at how easily my tears came. I was not ashamed now, and I believe God gave me tears to begin the healing process. But, oh, how often they came after my husband's funeral. Time seemed to stretch on endlessly. At the sight of my husband's clothing, his workbench with projects uncompleted, a picture of him, or at the memory of times together, the tears spilled out.

God alone knows how many widows cry themselves to sleep night after night or how many widowers sit and stare hour after hour, longing for the sound of the familiar voice and the gentle pressure of the loved hand. God, who knows, has given us the ability to sorrow.

Moment by moment, day by day, He guides us through the pain and sorrow. The comforting word, the necessary task, and sometimes a gentle rebuke all are His means of healing. In the Psalms we see how God is attentive to every detail of our life: "Put Your tears into Your bottle; are they not in Your book?" (Ps. 56:8).

Though Jesus wept and Abraham sorrowed, they followed the tears with acts of faith. God still has a purpose for those who grieve. He who gave us the ability to sorrow now will also give us the ability to smile again.

Today I was given the chance to counsel a younger wife, advising her to be patient with her husband. I wept with her as she wept. And the time of my own weeping became less.

Prayer

Thank You for tears, Father. Jesus was not ashamed to cry and You see my tears. You are the God of comfort. Give me a heart of compassion for others. In Jesus' name. Amen.

GRIEVING

The chair he always sat in
Sits right across from mine,
The book that he was reading
Marked at page eighty-nine.
It seems at any moment
He should walk in the door,
His smile and voice and chuckle
Same as it was before.
Oh, others try to tell me
The pain will ease and leave,
But right now I am grieving
And it's so hard to believe.
I sit and gaze at his chair,
I feel him sitting there.
I sense his love around me,
His voice is in the air.
Just let me sit awhile
For death is hard to bear.
And then I'll keep on living
As always, in God's care.

Learning to Be True

Through Your precepts I get understanding; therefore I hate every false way. (Psalms 119:104)

As I walked along the path on the dam above the lake, the aromatic scent of pine pervaded the air. The park department had strewn the mile-long trail with shredded Christmas trees brought to their collection areas after Christmas. If I closed my eyes, I could imagine myself in a dense pine forest. My open eyes dispelled such imaginings. For peaking through the shredded pine needles at my feet were tiny pieces of silvery tinsel, the remaining decorations from Christmas trees.

My Christmas tree was not part of this path. This year I put up the artificial one my husband and I bought some years ago. Now widowed and with all three sons in their own homes, I only buy a freshly cut tree the year all my family comes home for Christmas. That makes it special. I like the real tree best. I enjoy the fragrant aroma of pine in the house.

As I walked the pine-scented trail, I thought how the usefulness of the real tree had not ended but made the pathway pleasanter for all who walked or jogged along it.

"Make me like the real tree, Lord," I prayed silently. "Let my life in You be true with the real aroma of Christ in me."

The real tree begins with a tiny seed or cone. Our Christian life begins with the seed of faith God implants in our heart. Nurtured by rain and sun, the tree grows, strengthened by seasons that range from pleasant to harsh. We, too, need food for spiritual growth. We find it in God's Word. We experience joy, sorrow, and sometimes dark days of suffering. All are sent by God to strengthen and mature us.

Real trees grow.

Prayer

Dear Father, thank You for life and, most of all, life eternal.
Thank You for the nourishment You give me to grow
in You and for the pruning that often is necessary,
painful though it may be. In Jesus' name. Amen.

Learning to Be Like Him

*Beloved, now we are children of God; and it has
not yet been revealed what we shall be, but we know
that when He is revealed, we shall be like Him,
for we shall see Him as He is. (1 John 3:2)*

A magazine I used to read had a disconcerting way of putting pictures of people on its cover without the touchup most magazines use. Every blemish, freckle, and unflattering facial feature was clearly shown.

Most of us, I feel, prefer to see ourselves not "as we are" but "as we would like to be." I know I do, especially now that I've reached my three score years plus.

When a husband and wife grow old together, aging appears naturally and gradually. I miss my husband's assuring words as I moan over changes.

"I like that touch of silver in your hair," he'd say. "Don't touch it up."

And if I commented on how young a peer looked, he'd answer, "You look younger."

The eyes of love see differently from others.

God's eyes see us correctly. He sees us as sinners in need of a Savior, and He has provided His Son for our salvation. After we see ourselves as He does and accept His gift of salvation, He continues His work in our lives. He shows us our imperfections and, by His Holy Spirit, gives us the power to become more like Him.

We can't rid ourselves of all our imperfections in this earthly life, but He promises that someday we, His church, will stand before Him "not having spot or wrinkle . . . [but] holy and without blemish" (Eph. 5:27).

What a wonderful promise!

Prayer

Father, I thank You for the power of Your spirit in me to make me more like You. In Jesus' name. Amen.

Learning How to Rest

*But He Himself would often slip away to the
wilderness to pray. (Luke 5:16 NASB)*

*And He said to them, "Come away by yourselves
to a lonely place and rest a while." (For there were
many people coming and going, and they did not even
have time to eat.) (Mark 6:31 NASB)*

Our January thaw came the first week of February this
year. We had received more than fourteen inches of snow in
January, and the cold temperature kept it from melting.
Now, after five days of warm air, we saw the grass again.
Water flowed down the streets into the sewers.

I was tired after a busy morning but I forced myself to
go for a walk. As I strolled along, taking deep breaths of
the springlike air, I felt exhilarated and revived. Children
were playing outside in light coats and boots, making boats

out of sticks to sail on the miniature "rivers" along the curb. Snowmen, once firmly sculptured, were fast melting into small piles of snow marked by pieces of coal. Pleasant thoughts of my own childhood filled my mind. Weariness vanished. By the time I returned to my own front door, I felt rested.

I thought of how often, when I am physically tired, my mental attitude reacts negatively. I become cross and complaining and am easily provoked. How much better to turn aside from my busyness and rest or take a walk and feel God's renewing.

Jesus walked this earth in a physical body. He became tired and knew the importance of resting and being renewed in body, mind, and soul. He also taught us the importance of taking time to pray. Rest relaxes the body; prayer turns our thoughts to God, from whom we receive our daily strength.

Prayer

*Thank You, Creator of heaven and earth, for the renewed vigor
You give us when we turn aside from our tasks and
spend time with You, rejoicing in Your handiwork.
In Jesus' name. Amen.*

Learning That Morning Comes

*Weeping may endure for a night, but joy comes
in the morning. (Psalm 30:5)*

"Strong north winds and snow flurries continuing today, warmer and sunny tomorrow."

This was the weather forecast on the first day of spring.

I looked out my window at the gray, overcast skies and light skiff of snow gently covering the yellow daffodils.

"It will melt tomorrow if the forecast is correct," I said aloud to myself. I had seen this happen before.

"It will be better tomorrow," I would say to my sons when they were little, and I bandaged cuts and scrapes.

"But it hurts now," they would wail tearfully. The next

morning they were back at play, pain and tears gone and forgotten.

As parents, we spend many sleepless nights as we suffer through our children's illnesses and problems. We dispense medicine and watch over them. We pray and try to wait patiently.

Sometimes the night of weeping seems endless, and we think morning will never come. Some nights appear interminable because of the pain, but God has promised a morning, and His promises are sure. We walk by faith not by sight. Someday, all of the tears of this earthly walk will be over and we will shout with the joy of heaven.

Jesus reminded His disciples that "in the world you will have tribulation; but be of good cheer, I have overcome the world" (John 16:33).

Prayer

Nights are long and often so dark we cannot see. Give us eyes of faith, Father, to take us through the darkness into the glorious light of morning. Through Jesus our Lord. Amen.

Learning to Trust in God's Promises

For all the promises of God in Him are Yes,
and in Him, Amen. (2 Corinthians 1:20)

I filled my lungs with the fresh morning air. Already there was a touch of warmth in the breeze. As I stood on the back steps, a familiar sound drew my attention upward. Vividly etched against the gray morning sky, a wavering V-shaped line moved northward. Their incessant honking and graceful flight stirred an eager response from me. Geese were returning northward. True harbingers of spring!

When Noah and his family left the ark, God gave them and us a wonderful promise.

*"While the earth remains, seedtime and harvest,
and cold and heat, winter and summer, and day
and night shall not cease." (Genesis 8:22)*

As I watched the geese circle and turn in the direction of nearby lakes, my heart rejoiced in God's faithfulness.

Our Creator, who has set the seasons in order, has also promised eternal life to all who receive His Son, Jesus Christ, as Lord and Savior. He is faithful in all His promises.

Prayer

Thank You for a new day and a new season! Thank You for Your faithfulness. Keep me this day from allowing doubts and discouragement to hinder my service, Father. Guide my way through all the seasons of my life. In Jesus' name. Amen.

Learning Something New

A wise man will hear and increase learning,
and a man of understanding will attain
wise counsel. (Proverbs 1:5)

The young girl sacking my groceries looked closely at the potatoes.

"They didn't clean them very well when they dug them, did they?" she asked.

I suppressed a smile. "They're seed potatoes," I said.

"Oh!" She picked up the bags of onion sets, looked at them and then at me.

"Do you plant these too?" she asked hesitantly.

"Yes," I replied, my smile escaping this time. "You don't garden, do you?"

"No, but my mother does," she replied, returning my smile.

I chuckled to myself as I drove home, thinking how the young clerk had added to her knowledge that day. I remembered my early days of gardening. "Which way do I put these onion sets in the ground?" I asked my more knowledgeable husband and learned from his teasing reply. I remembered how he finally put stakes all around the pepper plants so I would stop pulling them up as weeds.

Life is full of learning! We learn from those who have already learned. Sometimes we learn from their successes; sometimes from their mistakes. God expects us to keep learning in our walk with Him, too.

"Take My yoke upon you, and *learn* from Me, for I am gentle and humble in heart" said Jesus (Matt. 11:29 NASB, emphasis added). Paul said, "For I have *learned* to be content in whatever circumstances I am" (Phil. 4:11 NASB, emphasis added).

Prayer

*Help me to be ever teachable that I may learn to be
more like You. In Jesus' name. Amen.*

Learning from the Birds

Even the sparrow has found a home, and the swallow
a nest for herself, where she may lay her young,
even Your altars, O LORD of hosts. (Psalm 84:3)

I stepped to my sink to wash a dish, and the goldfinch, perched on the feeder outside the window, took flight.

"Hey," I admonished, "who do you think put that food in your feeder? It was me!"

One tiny, bright yellow, black-capped finch returned and, with head cocked, watched me as he pecked on a thistle seed. I stood very still. Soon another came, hesitated, then began to peck away at the food in the plastic tube. I watched in delight, motionless, lest I frighten them away again.

I love watching the birds that frequent my backyard, too. Some stay all winter and brighten gray, snowy days as they gather on and under the bird feeder. The flashy red cardinals usually come when no other birds are there. The noisy, bossy blue jays take over when they appear. The shiny black starlings have learned to fly at the suet I've set in a wire holder. They knock some to the ground and fight over each scrap. The downy woodpecker clings to the wire holder and enjoys what is left. Sometimes a redheaded woodpecker comes and sometimes a larger flicker. The black-capped chickadees and sparrows busily eat the seed that has fallen to the ground.

Spring brings the welcome song of robins and the repetitious "feebe-feebe" of two tiny black and white birds perched on the branch of my hackberry tree. Brown thrashers return. Morning begins with a cheery song when the house wrens take up housekeeping in the little house in my elm. A bright flash of orange and melodious song announce the orioles.

"Hey," I say to myself, "who do you think created and sent these birds to brighten your days? Thank *You,* Father."

Prayer

Yes, thank You, heavenly Father, for all Your creation, reminding us of Your power and care. In Jesus' name. Amen.

Learning to Waste Not

When they were filled, He said to His disciples,
"Gather up the fragments that remain,
so that nothing is lost." (John 6:12)

Having been raised during the Depression of the thirties, I know what it means to "use it up, wear it out, make it do, or do without."

My parents always had a big garden. So did my husband's parents. So, when my husband and I moved from our small apartment to a house with land around it, we planted a garden. My experience has always been that gardens were for sharing with others as well as for supplying your own needs. If the green beans, tomatoes, or any crop kept producing after you put away enough for your use, you gave the rest away. Some crops go on and on. Many jokes have been told about zucchini, which produces abundantly.

People have been accused of putting their excess on neighbors' doorsteps during the night. A gardener simply cannot let his produce go to waste.

"Clean up your plate," admonished my mother. "Some starving child in this world would be glad to have this food." I repeated her words to my children when they were little.

Today I'm glad to see our country sending surplus food to starving people in other nations.

Living alone now, I try to plant only a small garden. Still, there is always enough to share. I've also joined the ranks of those who recycle old newspapers, plastic bottles, telephone books, and so forth. I make a compost pile and use the back of used paper for notes. Conservation is becoming more important to many people now, and I am glad to see young children learning to do their part in conserving instead of wasting.

Jesus didn't believe in waste. Neither should we.

Prayer

Father, help us not to be wasteful of anything
Your love has provided. Giver of every good gift,
we thank You. In Jesus' name. Amen.

Learning to Pray for Everything

Pray without ceasing. (1 Thessalonians 5:17)

"I pray for safety on long trips but I don't on little trips around town," a Christian gentleman once told me.

"I always wear my seat belt when we travel far, but I tend to forget when I have just a short way to go," another friend said.

I wondered, as I thought about their comments, if they had heard the National Safety Council's report on how many accidents happen within a short radius of our homes. In fact, many happen right in our homes.

It seems as if we feel God doesn't want to be bothered with little details and problems in our lives. So we only ask Him for help and guidance in big things. When our lives are in a turmoil and grave problems arise, we turn earnestly to Him in prayer.

The Bible says God is watching and thinking about us all the time. Psalm 139 is one of my favorite psalms. I read: "You know my sitting down and my rising up; You understand my thought afar off" (v. 2). And again, "How precious also are Your thoughts to me, O God! How great is the sum of them!" (v. 17).

"You Americans are so independent," says a Nigerian friend. "Back in Nigeria we do not hesitate to ask one another for help when we need it."

I flinched. I had been moaning about all the work I had to do. She reminded me that she had offered her help but I hadn't called to accept.

Jesus told us to "ask." His praying made the disciples beg Him to teach them to pray, and part of that prayer was, "give us this day our *daily* bread" (Matt. 6:11, emphasis added). He also said, "For without me you can do nothing" (John 15:5).

I'm learning to pray about everything. "Popcorn prayers," a friend calls them. But God always hears, and He answers. Prayer gives peace.

Prayer

We do need You every moment, Lord. That You want us
to come to You with everything is more than we can understand.
Thank You for hearing and answering our prayers.
In Jesus' name. Amen.

Learning As We Grow Older

*The days of our lives are seventy years; and if by
reason of strength they are eighty years, yet their boast
is only labor and sorrow; for it is soon cut off,
and we fly away. (Psalm 90:10)*

"Tomorrow, I'll be forty-nine. Imagine! Another year and I'll be fifty." Our walking companion's voice registered consternation at the thought of advancing years.

The male of our trio grinned. "Wow! She's really getting up there."

I grinned too. "She sure is," I agreed.

The almost-fifty looked at us with an embarrassed smile as she remembered. I was sixty-four, and he was seventy-one.

"It's funny," said seventy-one, "how the years past forty seem threatening at first. Then all of a sudden you reach seventy, and you feel happy to reach this age."

The conversation moved on to health and other subjects. After completing our three-mile walk (without any noticeable shortness of breath, I might add), I found myself contemplating the subject of age. Some use age as an excuse for physical and mental shortcomings. Others ignore the subject. What is the best way to face the advancing years?

I realize physical and mental health play an important part in the way we function. However, I have found much in God's Word regarding age to be a comfort, encouragement, and guide.

The psalmist tells of God giving people power in their old age to tell of His greatness and goodness. God used Abraham, Moses, Caleb, Joshua, Samuel, and Daniel (and the list goes on), all when they were older, to accomplish His purposes.

But God is the strength of my heart and my portion forever. (Psalm 73:26)
They shall still bear fruit in old age. (Psalm 92:14)

Prayer

Dear God, in whose hands are the times of our lives, I thank You for Your abiding Holy Spirit and Your many precious promises that assure me You will never forsake me. Let me bear fruit all the days of my life. In Jesus' name. Amen.

Learning to Be Patient

But the fruit of the Spirit is love, joy, peace, patience,
kindness, goodness, faithfulness, gentleness,
self-control. (Galatians 5:22–23 NASB)

The car in front of me was moving much more slowly than the speed limit required. This became increasingly irritating. Finally I muttered a disgusted, "If you don't know how to drive, get off the road."

My adult son seated beside me said quietly, "My friend, Bev, says our Christian spirit is truly tested when we drive."

It was a gentle rebuke, but it stung. It was true. Behind the wheel I seemed to be more impatient with others and have less respect for any physical limitation that might cause them to drive as they do. In this case, as I looked more closely at the driver in the car ahead, it was probably age. The man was obviously quite old and the tiny, white-haired lady sitting beside him seemed perfectly content to be moving at the speed they were traveling. They weren't in a hurry and felt perfectly safe proceeding slowly.

"I am impatient," I confessed to my son. "It's something else I need to pray about, besides safety, when I get behind the wheel."

For I usually do pray when I prepare to drive. It is a simple prayer. "Lord, keep me from harming others and keep me from harm as I travel."

I have seen an answer to this prayer. God has saved me many times from potentially dangerous situations. Because of His Holy Spirit, I can also bear the fruit of patience and self-control. Although it does not come naturally to me, I can learn to be patient with His help.

Prayer

Lord, when I'm driving, walking, talking, meditating;
at all times help me to abide in You that others may see You in
me. For as You have said, apart from You I cannot bear fruit.
In Jesus' name. Amen.

Learning from Friends

*A friend loves at all times, and a brother is born
for adversity. (Proverbs 17:17)*

It's sad to see friends move away. Sadder yet is the final good-bye at a friend's death. But their impact on your life remains.

Finding myself in the world of singles again after my husband's death brought me into relationships with others who were alone. From these new friends I learned ways to cope with my loneliness. Old friends are special, but it is important to make new friends.

Age is no barrier in friendships, I have found. For several years I was part of a group of people from my church who met weekly at the home of three single women. Men and women, we ranged in age from the early twenties to late seventies. We were a diverse group: married, divorced, widowed, single; college students, office workers, teachers, retired, homemakers. We laughed, cried, studied, discussed, and prayed together. We saw the young singles through unhappy romances and finally rejoiced with them when they found the "right one" and married. We sympathized and helped in times of illness. We welcomed the new babies of our young married couples. We remembered each others' birthdays and anniversaries. We became, as one of the older ladies so aptly put it, "a family." Even today, although we are no longer a group, we have a bond of friendship that is evident whenever we see each other or have "reunions."

How I appreciate the friends God has put in my life. It's been said that a friend knows all your faults but loves you just the same. This is the kind of love Jesus said we should have for one another when He told us to, "love one another as I have loved you" (John 15:12).

Friends have enriched my life. I thank God for each one of them.

Prayer

Father, I thank You that Jesus laid down His life for us and called us friends. Help me be the friend You want me to be. In Your precious name. Amen.

Learning to Be a Mother-in-Law

Older women likewise are to be reverent in their
behavior, not malicious gossips, nor enslaved to
much wine, teaching what is good, that they may
encourage the young women to love their husbands,
to love their children, to be sensible, pure, workers at
home, kind, being subject to their own husbands.
(*Titus 2:3–5* NASB)

I have often said that I think I would have been a better daughter-in-law if I could have been a mother-in-law first. But it doesn't work that way. I remember my mother-in-law's patience with me and pray that I may be a good mother-in-law, too.

An older lady I admire once said to me, "I call them daughters-in-love." I like that, and I know that her sons' wives did, too.

The book of Ruth is a good study on the relationship of a mother-in-law with her daughters-in-law. I have made a list for myself of the traits I saw in Naomi that made her sons' wives truly daughters-in-love.

1. Naomi lived a godly life before them.

2. She accepted and loved her sons' wives although they were of the Gentile, not Jewish, faith.

3. She was concerned for their welfare above her own.

4. She was not jealous of her daughters-in-law's parents and family.

5. She prayed for her two daughters-in-law and desired the best for them.

6. She showed appreciation for their acts of love and kindness shown to her and her sons.

7. Naomi was practical and wise in her advice.

8. She accepted Ruth's decision to go with her and was considerate of her welfare and future.

9. She loved and cared for Ruth and Boaz's son as her own.

Prayer

Father, may my daughters-in-love see Your Spirit in me.
Let my love for them be a love that is not jealous or critical;
let it be like Your love. I thank You for the wife You have given
to each of my three sons. Help me to be an encourager to them.
In Christ's name. Amen.

Learning That God Knows My Needs

And in their heart they put God to the test by asking food according to their desire. (Psalm 78:18 NASB)

"But I want it! I need it!" The little girl's cries of protest filled the store. Her mother quietly and firmly took the article from her child's hands and put it back on the counter. The little girl's protests became louder as she tearfully insisted, "But I *really* need it. I do."

I'm sure there were many of us in the store who were thinking that what the child *really* needed was a firm spanking. At the same time, we were feeling great compassion for the mother. Perhaps others were remembering, as I was, similar embarrassing moments in the past when one of our children had indulged in a public tantrum.

The insistent cries of the child came to my mind again that night as I read the above Scripture passage. This was the second time in as many days that I had been reminded by sermon or Scripture reading of the sinfulness of the Israelites as God led them through the wilderness. I was convicted of my own sin. I had believed God had failed to grant me a fervent desire, and I had cried out to Him in protest. He surely knew how much I *needed* to be granted this request.

God was meeting every need of the Israelites, but still they wanted more.

God was meeting my daily needs, and instead of being appreciative, I cried out for what I thought I needed for complete fulfillment. As I remembered how God had met my needs in the past (something the Israelites should have done), I bowed my head in contrite prayer. With thankfulness, I made my request to God, according to His will.

Prayer

Thank You, Father, for Your loving-kindness,
faithfulness, and forgiveness. I have been indulging
in a tantrum, here in my heart. You know what is best for me.
Give to me according to Your will. In Jesus' name. Amen.

Learning to Forgive

Let all bitterness, wrath, anger, clamor,
and evil speaking be put away from you,
with all malice. (Ephesians 4:31)

Late in my teens I came across a prayer that was meaningful to me. I have long ago lost the words, but my memory retains one line clearly: "Let me hide my little hurts and heartaches so that I am the only one affected by them."

I have a sensitive nature. Too sensitive, my friends say, gently rebuking me when I take offense at words or actions that have hurt me.

I have not always been successful in hiding all my little hurts so that I am the only one affected. Others have felt my anger and reproof. But the Lord has been convicting me lately on this. I feel His rebuke as I read His Word. "And just as you want people to treat you, treat them in the same way" (Luke 6:31 NASB). "Not returning evil for evil, or insult for insult . . ." (1 Peter 3:9 NASB).

"You are not responsible for others' actions, only your reactions," some wise person once said.

When I concentrate on my reactions, it makes a big difference. After all, I have the example of Jesus, who never returned evil to those who were unkind, even cruel, to Him. And He suffered much more from the words and actions of others than I ever have.

So often a gentle answer or a smile to someone who has spoken unkindly to you brings a surprised and repentant response.

A friend once told me, "You can't be angry at someone you are praying for." How true! God will give you empathy for that person and a forgiving spirit. Prayer also takes away your self-pity. It is self-pity that you are experiencing when you let insults affect you for any length of time. These small hurts can only affect you as much as you choose to let them.

Prayer

Today, I want to speak only kind and helpful words. If others treat me badly, help me to respond with love. I need Your help. Thank You. In Jesus' name. Amen.

Learning to Forget

As far as the east is from the west, so far has He removed our transgressions from us. (Psalm 103:12)

"How can I forgive her for the awful things she said about me," cried the young woman. "I thought she was my friend."

Yes, how? God can and will give us the ability to forgive, that I know. It's forgetting that's more difficult.

I thought I had wanted to know what someone said about me, but when I found out, I felt hurt and angry. How could someone I had trusted say such humiliating things about me? Or, so it seemed! When I presented her with my hurt, she was surprised. She hadn't meant it, she insisted, the way I had taken it. Still, we both knew our friendship was harmed. I felt she had betrayed my confidence.

I remembered what happened to Lucy in C. S. Lewis's *The Chronicles of Narnia*. Although Lucy knew she shouldn't, she had yielded to the spell of the magic book and learned what a friend was saying about her to someone else. Although the friend later said she hadn't meant what she'd said, Lucy told Aslan that, although she forgave her friend, she would never forget what she had heard.

Aslan quietly answered, "No, you won't."

How sad! How true! But God, who helps me forgive, can also help me forget. When the hurtful remembrance comes to mind, I will pray—and not let it dwell in my thoughts. I will try to recall that God remembers my sins no more after I have repented of them. They are forgiven *and* forgotten. If I am to be the older woman God has instructed me to be, I must forgive and *forget*.

Prayer

Father, I thank You that my sins are washed away by Jesus' blood shed for me. Fill me with a love like yours that does not bear grudges. In Jesus' name. Amen.

Learning to Be Thankful at All Times

In everything by prayer and supplication,
with thanksgiving, let your requests be made
known to God. (Philippians 4:6)

I first saw Jan as she whizzed by the door in her wheelchair. Later, when I met her in the hall, I had a closer look. Jan's room was across the hall in the nursing home where Mother had come to recuperate from surgery.

I guessed Jan to be in her twenties. She had dark brown, shoulder-length hair and large brown, expressive eyes. I noticed her eyes first before realizing that Jan did not have legs. She was born that way, I learned later. Once she had been able to walk with braces. Problems with her hips necessitated surgery. Now Jan was recuperating, waiting for the doctor's permission to resume the use of her braces. She zoomed along the corridors and visited with everyone she met, and she was always smiling. Then one day I met her in the hall, and she was not smiling. Her dark eyes were somber.

"My doctor says I may never walk again," she said.

What could I say? I murmured sympathetically and put my hand on hers.

"Have you ever heard of Joni Eareckson and her story?" I asked. Jan nodded. I went on. "She was paralyzed in a diving accident when she was seventeen. I've read that she can't even raise her hand to scratch her nose. You can scratch your nose, Jan." I playfully took her hand and placed it on her nose.

I was apprehensive. Were my words too preachy and flippant? But Jan was smiling again. "Yes, I can still do a lot of things," she said. "I can still embroider, read, and listen to my records."

And encourage others, I thought as she turned her wheel-chair into a nearby room to visit a lady lying in bed.

I have recalled my words to Jan many times when I have been discouraged.

"You can scratch your nose," I remind myself. And I smile.

Prayer

Thank You, Lord, for little blessings, even being able to scratch my nose. In Jesus' name. Amen.

Learning I Don't Need to Understand

A man's steps are of the LORD; how then can a man understand his own way? (Proverbs 20:24)

I had enjoyed good health most of my life. My three pregnancies had been fairly easy and without complications. They were my only time in a hospital except for having a bunion removed (a short stay).

Now the doctor said surgery.

It was cancer. One of the most curable varieties. Still, the word came as a shock.

One of my first reactions was wishing my husband was with me. He, who had known so many days in the hospital and surgery so much more serious, would have comforted me. Why must I go through this now, as a widow? Why, when I had always been so healthy, was this happening to me?

The "whys" piled up in my mind. That night, as I opened my Bible to the wisdom of Proverbs, I came to verse 24 of chapter 20. I read it over and over. Could I have never read it before? It spoke to me now. God was answering my "whys" by telling me I didn't need to understand. He was in control.

Then I turned to the precious words of Philippians 4:6–7: "Be anxious for nothing, but in everything by prayer and supplication with thanksgiving let your requests be made known to God. And the peace of God, which surpasses all comprehension, shall guard your hearts and your minds in Christ Jesus" (NASB).

Two days later I had my surgery. The doctors pronounced it a success but wanted me to take twenty-two days of radiology for added precaution. I agreed. The peace that passed all understanding was still with me.

Prayer

God of peace, I know now my own understanding is not sufficient. Thank You for the peace You give when I take everything to You in prayer. In Jesus' name. Amen.

Learning from Others' Afflictions

*It is good for me that I have been afflicted, that
I may learn Your statutes. (Psalm 119:71)*

My neighbor is fighting a battle with cancer. She is only thirty-eight and has a husband and three sons. The oldest son is seventeen and very solicitous of his mother. The fourteen-year-old twins are quiet, not sure how to react to their mother's illness. She worked outside the home before her illness but now is at home all day. The sons are very aware of their mother's reaction to pain, distress, and problems.

She is concerned about that.

"I'm afraid my sons do not always see me victorious or rejoicing in the Lord," she says.

"But they see you turning to His Word for comfort and guidance," I replied.

That is true. She starts the difficult mornings with her Bible. Again at midday she is often reading the Word, finding help and hope in God's precious promises. Her pastor comes once a week. Others come, too, and they study the book of Job together. All this her sons are observing.

In the time I spend walking and talking with her, I see how she is learning more and more to lean on the Lord for strength. God's Word is vital to her daily walk. She finds help in every shared testimony of God's power in the lives of others.

I feel humble in her presence. I, too, have known the help that only God's Word can give in trials. Still, I am not walking in the "valley of the shadow of death" as she is. I am learning from her.

Prayer

Our Father, thank You for my neighbor's witness to me and others. Thank You for the work of Your Holy Spirit I see in her. Bless her, Lord, and Your will be done in her life and in that of her family. In Jesus' name. Amen.

Learning Humility

Therefore let him who thinks he stands take heed lest he fall. (1 Corinthians 10:12)

My new friend fairly bubbled over as she told me of the joy she had found. She had finally understood that living the Christian life did not mean striving and struggling on her part, but simply looking to God for guidance and trusting Him to work in and through her.

"Not that I've arrived yet," she hastily added. "You don't arrive until you get there."

I was glad our conversation was taking place over the telephone, as she might not have understood my sudden desire to laugh. It was not at the humor of what she said but the simple truth said so effectively.

"We don't arrive until we get there." Of course not.

Not in our earthly walk nor in our spiritual, heavenward walk.

We would be foolish to say, halfway on a journey, that we had arrived. Similarly, we are warned as Christians never to consider ourselves as "having arrived."

Paul writes in Philippians 3:13, "Brethren, I do not regard myself as having laid hold of it yet; but one thing I do: forgetting what lies behind and reaching forward to what lies ahead" (NASB).

Our Christian life consists in pressing on; never arriving here on earth but being assured that some day, "We shall be like Him, for we shall see Him as He is" (1 John 3:2).

Prayer

More like You, Father, I would be, and help me
never to think more highly of myself than I should.
In Christ's name. Amen.

Learning to See and Hear

Though now you do not see Him, yet believing,
you rejoice with joy inexpressible and full of glory.
(1 Peter 1:8)

As I read the Gospels, I often wonder what it would have been like to walk with Jesus as He traveled throughout Judea and walked by the Sea of Galilee. How sweet it would have been to hear His voice as we walked.

But as I take my evening walk along the dam above the lake, I remind myself that He *is* with me. For He abides in me and I in Him. I have His Word to instruct and teach me as I think on it while I walk.

If I am struggling with a fleshly weakness, I remember, "For we do not have a high priest who cannot sympathize with our weaknesses, but one who has been tempted in all things as we are, yet without sin" (Heb. 4:15 NASB).

If troubles and trials are making me anxious and weary, I obey His words, "Casting all your care upon Him, for He cares for you" (1 Peter 5:7).

A meadowlark bursts into melodic song a few feet ahead of me beside the path. As I draw near, I see a glimpse of yellow breast and throat as he flies off with a whir of wings. A fish jumps out in the middle of the lake. A pair of mallard ducks cross the lake with their young. The Creator of heaven and earth is seen in all He has created. He walks and talks with me through His Word and His creation.

All things were made through Him, and without Him nothing was made that was made. (John 1:3)

Prayer

I cannot touch You, Lord, or see You or hear Your voice, but Your creation makes You known and Your Holy Spirit opens my eyes and ears to understand. In Jesus' name. Amen.

Learning About Daily Bread

"It is written, 'Man shall not live by bread alone,
but by every word that proceeds from the mouth
of God.'" (Matthew 4:4)

I baked bread today. I hadn't baked bread for quite a while. It didn't seem necessary now that my husband wasn't here to cut the first slice while it was still warm.

"That isn't good for you," I'd admonish.

"But it's best warm," he'd grin, as he eagerly bit into the slice he had buttered.

It was almost a ritual; my admonition and his answer. And I missed it.

But today I decided to bake bread. It had been a bitterly cold week, with ice and snow. I had cleaned house, washed clothes, and now I wanted to bake something. Also, my parents would enjoy homemade rolls from part of the dough. My oldest son and his two children were coming for dinner while their wife-mom was out of town. I also thought of a neighbor who had experienced a recent sorrow. They might appreciate a loaf; so I made my dough. As I kneaded, I glanced out the window occasionally at the birds flocking around my feeder. The little juncos busily ate the seeds the sparrows, perched on the feeder, were scattering to the ground.

"Give us this day our daily bread" we pray, and God does. But this does not mean bread such as I was baking now. It means all our daily needs—food for our soul as well as our body—the beauty of God's creation, the blessing of family and friends, the privilege and ability to share with others, and thankfulness for all things.

The aroma of freshly baked bread still filled the house when my family arrived. Appetites were soon satisfied and the bread was eaten eagerly. I was glad I'd baked bread today.

Prayer

Each day You supply our daily bread. You supply all our needs.
Help me to live relying on You in faith and obedience to
Your Holy Word. In Jesus' name. Amen.

Learning Alertness

Be on the alert, stand firm in the faith, act like men,
be strong. (1 Corinthians 16:13 NASB)

The defense sirens sounded their weekly warning. If I hadn't known before, I would know now that it was 10:15, Wednesday morning. I had become so accustomed to this weekly testing of the sirens that I hardly noticed it. It was only when the sirens followed a different order of blasts or came at a different time that I would heed their warning. Then I would know a tornado was heading in our direction, and we were to take cover.

If we were to be attacked by an enemy, Wednesday morning at 10:15 would be an excellent time, I thought. Even that thought failed to alarm me. Situated as we were in the central part of the United States, an enemy would need to evade the coastal warning systems set up during World War II, before reaching us.

We can become oblivious to warnings. Jesus said, "For those days will be a time of tribulation such as has not occurred since the beginning of the creation which God created, until now, and never shall" (Mark 13:19 NASB). Again, Paul, in his letter to the Thessalonians warned, "For you yourselves know full well that the day of the Lord will come just like a thief in the night" (1 Thess. 5:2 NASB).

Just as in Paul's day, many today laugh at these warnings. But God's Word is true. As our defense systems continue to operate faithfully, so God's Word continues to warn us to be alert and faithful in making known His word and attending to it.

As the defense sirens faded away, I was thankful it was only a test. I wasn't prepared for the real thing. But I am prepared for the return of Christ through faith in Him and His provision for my salvation.

Prayer

Today, Lord, You may return. Let me live in readiness, prayerfully doing what is pleasing to You. Open many hearts to hear and believe Your Word today.
I pray in Jesus' name. Amen.

Learning to Care for Aged Parents

And Israel said to Joseph, "I never expected to see your face, and behold, God has let me see your children as well." (Genesis 48:11 NASB)

"I never thought when I was carrying you around as a baby that sixty-five years later you would be taking me places," my father said thoughtfully.

I glanced at him and smiled.

"Yes, we can't know, can we?" I agreed.

At eighty-eight and a half years of age, Dad had given up driving. His declining health made him realize that it was no longer wise for him to be behind the wheel. Because I lived near my parents, I became their main chauffeur. I know it was hard for Dad to accept this new position, but I had never heard him voice his feelings quite this way before. He was ninety now, and I realized that he had reached a place of thankful resignation. He was glad to have children to help him, just as he had cared for them in the past.

Jacob (Israel) had not realized that the son he loved and cared for would some day be providing for his needs in his old age. Joseph honored his father by doing so.

Jesus scolded the Pharisees and scribes for their tradition which negated the commandment about honoring their parents (Matt. 15:4–6). On the cross, Jesus turned the care of His mother over to His beloved disciple, John.

Reversing our caring roles of parent and child is difficult in many ways but can teach us to have more patience, love, and humility.

Prayer

Father, thank You for what You are teaching me in this changing relationship with my parents. Give me more of Your patience and love and thankfulness as I serve them the way they once cared for me. In Jesus' name. Amen.

Learning to Show Friendliness

A man who has friends must himself be friendly.
(Proverbs 18:24)

A new sign in front of a house on the slope above me caught my eye as I took my daily walk. The bold, black letters seemed to shout the words they formed: "Private Property. No Trespassing."

The sign seemed unnecessary. A dense hedge circled the property. As I walked by, I heard dogs barking from somewhere behind the house. The house obviously had protection from trespassers.

I moved on. I had no intention of disobeying the sign. I had been taught as a child to respect other people's property.

A young man visiting our country from Liberia once

commented to me about the obsession Americans seem to have with privacy. I wondered as I recalled his words, did he see "No Trespassing" signs on us as he tried to get to know us? We can put on a façade of politeness and friendliness, but if we never invite people into our homes and let them share our lives, aren't we putting up a sign that says, "Keep Out"?

Inviting strangers and new acquaintances into our home has been an enriching experience for our family. It has also been a way to combat loneliness since I became a widow. When a young singing group performed at our church, housing was needed. I volunteered and received two young women as guests for the night and breakfast. Their friendly chatter turned an evening, which otherwise I would have spent alone, into a cheerful, pleasant time with new friends.

We all need some privacy. "No Trespassing" signs have their place. But a "Welcome" mat on our doorstep encourages visiting.

Prayer

Thank You, Lord, that there are no "No Trespassing"
signs keeping us from coming to You. Let Your love shine
through me onto others. In our Savior's name. Amen.

Learning to Observe

The heavens declare the glory of God; and the firmament shows His handiwork. (Psalm 19:1)

My father-in-law used to say, "I love to look at the sky. It's always changing." As he grew older asthma had slowed him down, and he found it necessary to sit and rest more often. Many times I'd find him sitting on a bench outdoors, looking skyward.

I had always enjoyed the beauty of the sky, too, but I hadn't reflected as he had on the changes. Now I did. Some mornings as I worked outside I enjoyed a bright, blue, cloudless sky where the sun was king. In a few hours, puffy cumulus clouds would begin to pile up from the horizon, rising higher and changing shape as they moved across the sky. I remembered as a child how we children would lie on our backs looking at the clouds. The little ones were lambs frisking across the sky, while others were big sticks of cotton candy. A cloud that, at first, looked like an old bearded man could soon change to a huge grizzly bear. The changing sky was our entertainment.

From a sheltered vantage point, I love to watch storm clouds gather and see them suddenly outlined by flashes of lightning. I wonder. The psalmist said, "He makes the clouds His chariot" (Ps. 104:3 NASB). I am awed by the thought of God riding in the dark clouds boiling up from the horizon.

Day and night, the sky reveals God's glory. I have stood at night where no man-made lights were shining and gazed up at a star-filled sky, so brilliant and sparkling I could only gasp in delight.

"If heaven is this beautiful on our side, what must it be like on God's side?" I wonder.

The sky changes. But the One who created it never changes. "Jesus Christ is the same yesterday, today, and forever" (Heb. 13:8).

Prayer

Father, when life is changing all around me, help me to keep my eyes fixed on You. In Jesus' unchanging name. Amen.

Learning to Wait

*Wait for the L*ORD*; be strong, and let your heart take courage; yes, wait for the L*ORD*. (Psalm 27:14 NASB)*

"Hurry! Hurry! Hurry!" the lady with an armful of papers moaned as she stepped on the elevator and punched the button for the top floor.

"I know what you mean," agreed a harried-looking hospital worker stepping in beside her. "That's all I've done today."

I listened to them share complaints, and I thought of how my day had mainly been spent in waiting, not hurrying.

Waiting. Waiting. Waiting.

As I stepped out of the elevator at my floor, the two ladies were still commiserating.

Which is harder, I wondered, waiting or hurrying? I have known days of both kinds. I remember days with so much to do that I fell exhausted into bed at night. I also recall times of waiting while a loved one had surgery (as I was about to do now), waiting in emergency rooms, waiting in stalled traffic; the list could go on. Waiting is difficult!

Reading my Bible during times of trial, I seemed always to come across reading admonitions to "wait." At first I rebelled at the words. Then I realized that the word *wait* was followed by *on the Lord.* God wasn't simply saying to "wait" but to "wait on Him." "But Those who wait on the LORD shall renew their strength . . ." (Isa. 40:31).

Waiting on the Lord gives me more time for prayer and reading His Word. I carry reading material with me for waiting times. Even waiting in line can lead to conversations that give you an opportunity to share your hope in God. I am learning to think of waiting as God's purpose for me. While I wait on Him, He is working out His perfect design for my life.

Prayer

Thank You, Father, that even in times of waiting You are there. It's not as hard to wait when I realize You are with me. In Christ. Amen.

Learning Tongue Control

Therefore, my beloved brethren, let every man
be swift to hear, slow to speak, slow to wrath.
(James 1:19)

I've often read in God's Word that there is a "time to keep silence, and a time to speak" (Eccl. 3:7), but I have trouble knowing the difference! I need help to obey the Lord's instructions to be "swift to hear, slow to speak, slow to wrath." Sometimes I fail. And sometimes I hurt others in the process.

Being sorry cannot always undo the harm done by hasty words. At times, I find I must go to the Father in prayer, asking Him to heal the hurt and give the one to whom I spoke a forgiving heart. And I need to ask God for His forgiveness, too.

Prayer

*Thank You, Father, for hearing and forgiving me now.
Please help me to put a guard on my lips and grow through
my mistakes. Help me to learn to control my tongue
and my thoughts. Let my speech become more gracious
and kind. In Your Son's name I ask. Amen.*

Learning Not to Procrastinate

So teach us to number our days, that we may
gain a heart of wisdom. (Psalm 90:12)

I had been promising myself for too long that I would go see her.

I'd pass the apartment building where she lived and sigh. I was always in a hurry, due someplace in a few minutes.

Then she died. Remorse filled my heart.

"I *will* stop putting off the things I should do," I vowed.

And with God's help I have tried. I visited an older friend the day before she passed away unexpectedly. We had such a good visit, and I was glad I had gone before it was too late. A little later, I enjoyed a good visit with another older friend a few days before a stroke rendered her incapable of communicating. In a few weeks, she too had died.

As I grow older, I realize more and more the importance of not putting off until tomorrow what I can do today. I am becoming more careful not to make rash promises. I pray earnestly for direction each day in all that I do. It doesn't always mean I am to keep each moment of the day filled with things to do. Sometimes it is spending more time in searching the Scriptures and praying than I usually do in my quiet time. Promises to pray for others are not to be taken lightly, I remind myself. Nor are promises to visit someone. Forgiving a hurt, confessing a fault, speaking a kind word, writing a letter—these things should not be put off. By prayerfully doing the things that God is putting on your heart right away, you can spare yourself the agony of saying, "I was too late. Too late!"

Prayer

*Lord, keep teaching me, as the moments add up to days
and the days to years, to realize that what I can do now
may not be possible tomorrow. In Jesus' name. Amen.*

Learning Through the Seasons

"While the earth remains, seedtime and harvest,
and cold and heat, and winter and summer, and day
and night shall not cease." (Genesis 8:22)

I love to see the seasons change. In Nebraska they often overlap. The first day of spring may come with snow covering the crocuses and early blooming daffodils. But one day you awaken to the pungent smell of stirring life in the earth around you. Spring is here! The days lengthen and temperatures climb higher. Lightning streaks across the sky and thunder rumbles as a thunderstorm announces the approach of summer. Parks and swimming pools fill as people throng to escape the heat rising from concrete streets.

Summer evenings call for long walks on shaded paths and beside lakes where others are also strolling. Leisurely days that all too soon wane. Glorious sunsets come earlier each evening. Summer birds leave, trees begin to show rust, orange, and yellow-colored leaves. The apple harvest begins, and farmers are busy in the fields all day.

Perhaps it's because I'm in what writers call the autumn of my life that I savor crisp fall days. I can take autumn vacations and enjoy a slower pace now that garden and yard work are decreasing. Time is precious, and I bask in the changes of autumn, knowing that my own body is undergoing changes as I grow older.

Many older people dread winter, when cold and ice keep them indoors. Or they flee, if circumstances and finances permit, to the warmer climes of our country. However, I enjoy the first snowfall. I stand at the window and watch the feathery flakes gently pile up outdoors. I do not look forward to ice and bitter cold north winds. I shovel snow more reluctantly each year, often gladly turning the chore over to younger hands. But winter follows fall and must be lived through before spring comes again. Lord willing, it will come!

Prayer

Father, I'm glad to know that, as Your hand rules over nature, so also our time is in Your hands. Help me to live each season of life in a way that is pleasing to You. In Jesus' precious name. Amen.

Learning As a Widow

*Now she who is a widow indeed, and who has
been left alone has fixed her hope on God,
and continues in entreaties and prayers
night and day. (1 Timothy 5:5 NASB)*

Today was a day of remembering. I suppose it always will be for me. July 7 is the day my husband went to be with the Lord. I relive again our last moments together, as we prepared to go fishing with our son and his wife. My husband had helped me adjust the rubber boots I had borrowed. He helped push the boat to the water's edge on the rocky beach in Alaska. Before we could get in the boat, he collapsed. Our daughter-in-law and another man ably administered CPR while an ambulance was summoned. As I prayed at the beach, I felt the strong arm of a man around me and heard him saying, "You must be brave."

I held my husband's hand all the way to the hospital but there was no familiar answering squeeze. He was gone.

I cry again, although I know the passing years have eased the pain. Time does heal even this most bitter pain.

Yes, I've gone on living and fixed my hope on God, as I'm sure many another widow has. God has given me a purpose as I serve others and do what He has for me to do. My husband left me and our sons good memories, and I do not grieve without the hope that Jesus gave to us, "For if we believe that Jesus died and rose again, even so God will bring with Him those who sleep in Jesus" (1 Thess. 4:14).

Prayer

Father, I thank You for love that grew through our years
of marriage. Thank You for Your love helping and sustaining
me through tearful nights and lonesome days. As I go on living,
let my life be one of service to You and others.
In Christ Jesus. Amen.

Learning in Awe

Praise the LORD! Praise God in His sanctuary;
praise Him in His mighty firmament!
(Psalm 150:1)

Clouds were settling down in Lake Clark Pass. I glanced at the pilot seated beside me. He was deftly handling the controls and seemed calm and confident as he had on my first flight two years ago to my son and daughter-in-law's Alaska wilderness cabin.

"I love coming back here," he said, and I smiled in agreement.

My first time had left an unforgettable impression on my mind. I had been apprehensive when my son told me of the narrowness of the pass. But fear was soon replaced by amazement and delight as we flew over the gray waters of Cook Inlet and the contorted channels of the tidal flats.

Then the scene changed to dense spruce and alder forests rising up the mountainside. Massive glaciers lay between the mountains, and waterfalls tumbled down from their lofty heights. Milky water formed channels below. We spotted moose near rocky spits of spruce-covered islands. Blessed with sunny skies I took many pictures. On our return trip, we flew over the pass instead of through it, and again I gasped in wonder as I filmed the snow-covered mountains and turquoise lakes lying like jewels below us.

The words of the hymn "How Great Thou Art" were ringing in my mind. Yes, how great Thou art, my God, I thought, as I reveled at the splendor all around me.

"It is I who made the earth, and created man upon it," says the Lord (Isa. 45:12 NASB).

His handiwork truly glorifies its creator. Do I, also His creation, glorify Him?

Prayer

Thank You, Lord, for the beauty You have given us in Your creation. I, too, want to reflect You in my life. Help me to do so. In Jesus' name. Amen.

Learning More of God's Creation

He has made everything beautiful in its time.
(Ecclesiastes 3:11)

A tap on my bedroom door roused me from a deep sleep. It was two o'clock in the morning. I heard my second son's voice saying, "Come, Mom, and see the northern lights."

In all my visits to my son's home in Alaska, I had never seen the northern lights. I quickly grabbed my robe and hurried to the big window downstairs. Across the sky white streaks of light were shimmering, rising, spreading, and then disappearing as other bright streaks of light appeared. It was as if I was watching the folds of a bluish white curtain being pulled across a huge stage before my eyes. I stood, transfixed, until at last they faded away entirely.

"That may be all tonight," my son said.

"Thank you for waking me," I whispered. "This will be one of the highlights of this trip, I know."

As always, I was taking home beautiful memories from my vacation in Alaska. Memories of rugged mountains pointing to the sky; large lakes reflecting the pines around them; waterfalls cascading to narrow canyons; cow moose and young feeding in a marsh; flowers—yellow, blue, red— marking my path in alpine meadows, and tall fireweed blooming around deserted log cabins. There was so much beauty even in the minutest dogwood blossom along a forest trail.

I realize that all around me, every day, I can see and enjoy what God has created. The spectacular display of the northern lights reminded me how God's glory is manifested in His handiwork.

Prayer

Father, Creator, help me to remember that I, too, have been created to glorify You. Let me worship You in the beauty of holiness. In Jesus' name. Amen.

Learning to Accept Rejection

"You have circled this mountain long enough.
Now turn north." (Deuteronomy 2:3 NASB)

I kept pondering the situation over and over again.
"What have I done wrong? Is there something wrong
with me? Why don't they like me?"

I tortured myself with these and similar thoughts until
each day became marred by my thinking.

Making new friends as a widow is not always easy, but
it is necessary. It's not always comfortable to be in the company of couples. Even with old friends, you feel you are an
extra person. As time goes on, God puts new people into
your life. They may not all become friends. I knew I should
have been grateful for the people who had become new and

dear friends. And I was! But not all new acquaintances would develop into friends, and the reasons were not intended to be insulting. I was making myself miserable by imagining, and I knew God wasn't pleased with me.

Casting all your care upon Him, for He cares for you. (1 Peter 5:7)

In all your ways acknowledge Him, and He shall direct your paths. (Proverbs 3:6)

As always, when I turned to the Word of God I was corrected and instructed. Like the children of Israel, I had been complaining and unhappy because God hadn't worked certain situations out in the way I wanted. My thinking was going in circles.

When I admitted that it was only my pride that was hurt, I was both ashamed and relieved. Repentance followed, and I put the rejection behind me. Many other acquaintances did become my friends, and I moved ahead in my life.

Prayer

Thank You, Father, for Your reproof and Your forgiveness. Help me to take my eyes off myself and to focus them on You at all times. In Jesus' name. Amen.

Learning About Waiting

*But those who wait on the L*ORD *shall renew
their strength; they shall mount up with wings like
eagles, they shall run and not be weary,
they shall walk and not faint. (Isaiah 40:31)*

Lord, I hate waiting!

Yet I read in Your Word, "Those who wait on the LORD
shall renew their strength."

WAITING

To me
waiting
is
wearying

But wait,
You say,
"Wait on the LORD!"

So, when I must wait, Lord,
Direct my thoughts to You,
To Your will in the waiting,
That I may be strengthened.

I see now
waiting
is good for me.
It slows me down,
Makes me see,
Without You I can do nothing.

Lord,
I hate to wait
Without You.

Prayer

Father, help me learn to wait on You with grace and patience.
In Jesus' name. Amen.

Learning of God's Willingness

Then He spoke a parable to them,
that men always ought to pray and not lose heart.
(Luke 18:1)

I have a motto hanging by my telephone that reads, "God is greater than any problem I have."

I needed that reminder often after I was widowed and when I chose to stay in our home of twenty-eight years. Maintenance problems were bound to occur. Since my husband had always taken care of household repairs, I knew very little about coping with them.

With my son's help, I bought a new lawn mower when our very old one finally proved "unfixable." The new one worked fine for a long time. Then one day it simply wouldn't start. Now what? The shop where I had purchased the mower had moved across town. They charged a large fee to pick up and deliver. I pondered and prayed. God already had the answer. One of my son's friends had a neighbor who repaired lawn mowers at home. He lived fairly close to me. He came and picked up my mower in his truck and soon had it back ready to use.

"I'll come get it when you've mowed for the last time this fall," he said. "I can sharpen your blades and get it ready for winter storage." And he did!

This was only one of many times God provided the help I needed. I keep learning to pray about everything. God knows my problems before I ask, but He says we are to ask.

"I don't bother God with my little problems," a lady once told me.

"He must not consider it a bother," I replied. "He answers."

He also says, "In everything give thanks" (1 Thess. 5:18).

Prayer

Yes, Father, You are greater than any of my problems and willing to answer when I ask. I thank You in Jesus' name. Amen.

Learning to Listen

The hearing ear and the seeing eye, the LORD has made both of them. (Proverbs 20:12)

Let every man be swift to hear, slow to speak, slow to wrath. (James 1:19)

"Mommy," the little girl said, "look at me when I'm talking to you."

I smiled at the little girl's pleading, but I was thinking that even a little child knows when you are not really listening.

I'm *learning* to listen. I've always been a daydreamer and, too often, my mind picks up a few words of a conversation and wanders off on thoughts they've inspired. Or worse yet, I listen but I'm thinking more about what I'm going to say next than what the other person is saying.

A popular adage reminds us, "God gave us two ears but only one tongue."

Listening requires a heart of understanding. Most of us need someone to listen to us with an attentive, caring attitude.

Ever since my parents went into a nursing home, I've come to understand how important listening is. Some of the residents in the home do not speak rationally, but their faces brighten up when an aide or nurse listens to them and talks to them. Many are lonely; to have someone listen to them brightens their day.

The greatest listener we have is always available. The psalmist says, "O You who hear prayer, to You all flesh will come" (Ps. 65:2). "I cried out to God with my voice—to God with my voice; and He gave ear to me" (Ps. 77:1).

God listens and answers wisely.

Prayer

Father, I want to be a good listener. Guard my tongue and keep me from interrupting others, for You know my weakness. In Jesus' name. Amen.

Learning to Let God Steer

Whoever loves discipline loves knowledge, but he who hates reproof is stupid. (Proverbs 12:1 NASB)

"She's rowing her boat with both oars on the same side of the boat."

The man sighed as he said these words. His wife had long been a person who liked to keep busy. Now she had been slowed down by a heart problem. The doctor's orders were to rest, but she was finding it difficult to obey.

I didn't quite understand her husband's description of the situation until I talked to my second son and his wife. They are both excellent boaters.

"If you're rowing with both of your oars on the same side of the boat," they told me, "you'll go in circles. You won't get anywhere."

I nodded. Now I understood. That was exactly what I

was doing when I was unwilling to accept changes in my life. I wanted perfect health for my husband. I wanted life to return to the regular schedule we once had. I was getting nowhere until I cried, "Lord, You know I want to pray for my desires. Nevertheless, not my will but Yours be done."

That was how I learned that, when two people are rowing a boat, they must row in harmony, so they will go forward. When I let God be the captain of my life's boat, while I sit in the stern and follow directions, the boat begins moving ahead. Under God's direction, when the rowing seemed the most difficult, my husband was sent to Minneapolis Veterans' Hospital for open-heart surgery. Twenty more years of life followed.

I prayed that the lady rowing with both oars on the same side of her boat would learn to give God one of the oars and let Him be captain. He alone knows the way that is best for us.

Prayer

God, I thank You for putting my life's boat on the course that leads to eternal life through Your Son, our Savior. Amen.

Learning to Pause and Observe

Jesus therefore, being wearied from His journey,
sat thus by the well. It was about the sixth hour.
(John 4:6)

"Resting is not idleness," the elderly man said to me. "Hmm!" I pondered his words. There was wisdom there, I was sure. In this busy, busy world, we are often made to feel that if we are not "doing something" all the time, we are being idle or, more bluntly, "lazy." I am learning that resting is necessary and refreshing. Even a few moments in the midst of labor can make work more pleasurable.

This morning I hoed furiously at the weeds that were growing profusely in my vegetable garden after our many rains. It was cool while the sun was low in the sky, and I wanted to accomplish much. Birds sang around me, and butterflies flitted from flower to flower. Head down, I chopped away at the weeds. The cheery, trilling song of the house wren was prompting answering trills from the bushes next to my garden fence. Their persistent song finally made me look up. Two wrens flew by me, lighting on a nearby bush. The sounds continued from inside the branches of the bush. I walked closer, stopped, and waited. Soon I saw a tinier wren move higher in the bush, then another and another.

"Oh," I exclaimed, "the baby wrens have left their nest."

How nice to have more of these cheery birds around. Every spring I looked forward to the first song that announced the wrens' return. Now there would be more glad songs. I watched them as they flitted from branch to branch, singing all the while. With a smile, I returned to my hoeing. It didn't seem so formidable now.

The dictionary describes *idleness* as "habitually doing nothing; lazy." *Resting* is defined as "refreshing ease or inactivity after exertion or labor." Resting is part of God's plan for humankind and nature. As Jesus rested He witnessed to a Samaritan woman.

Prayer

Thank You, Father, for times of rest. May even these times serve Your purpose for my life. In our Savior's name. Amen.

Learning As an Older Grandmother

*"And may he be to you a restorer of life
and a nourisher of your old age." (Ruth 4:15)*

Becoming a grandmother again at sixty-four posed some questions. Would I have the energy I had thirteen years ago when my first grandson was born? Could I help care for this new grandson as I had my first? His grandfather was alive to share our grandparenting privileges then. What would it be like now?

At Aaron's six-month birthday I can report Grandma is doing fine. She welcomes each opportunity to care for her new grandson. And she still bowls, bicycles, plays miniature golf, and goes on long walks with her fourteen-year-old grandson and ten-year-old granddaughter.

I thank God for health and strength to enjoy my grandchildren. I am reminded of our sons' older grandmother. She gave birth to my husband when she was forty-three. I can still recall how our youngest son, when he was four, would bring all his favorite reading books and put them in his grandma's lap. With infinite patience, she read them over and over to him. She wasn't too old to enjoy being a grandmother although she wasn't physically active anymore. She did what she was able to do, and her grandchildren enjoyed her participation in their lives.

MY NEW GRANDSON

You gave us concern
Before you were born.
Your mother must rest
To go her full term.
But now you are here,
Mom and son are fine,
I say, "Thank You, God
For this grandson of mine."

Prayer

Thank You, Father, for the privilege of being a grandparent.
May my life help point my grandchildren to faith
in Christ Jesus, our Lord. Amen.

Learning About Love

We love Him because He first loved us. (1 John 4:19)

"This is true love," said Robert as he opened his lunch pail. "Yeah," agreed his friend, Ralph, eyeing the contents of Robert's wedge-shaped dish. "Pumpkin pie!"

"No!" said Robert, "Pumpkin pie *with whipped cream.*" And he opened a separate plastic container filled with a generous helping of whipped cream topping.

I'm sure a piece of his favorite pie assured Robert of his wife's love. The whipped topping made him feel extra special. Love has a way of doing a little more than is expected.

Several years ago, when my husband was in the hospital on my birthday, I felt blue. We usually did something special in the evening. But, after spending the afternoon with him, I was now at home with our three young sons. They were playing before bedtime as I watched them. The doorbell rang. There stood a neighbor with a beautiful German chocolate cake.

"My mother baked it for you," she said.

"How did you know it was my birthday?" I gasped.

She smiled mysteriously but only queried about my husband's health and wished me a happy birthday.

"Tell your mother how much I appreciate her thoughtfulness," I said. Tears were forming. I was deeply moved by the kind act of a lady I had not met yet. She was visiting her daughter, my neighbor.

I still don't know how she knew it was my birthday. She couldn't have known my preference for chocolate cake! I have not forgotten her act of love.

Prayer

Thank You for love that reflects the love You have for us, Father, the love that results in action. Fill my heart with this love. In Christ. Amen.

Learning Not to Rely on Feelings

*These things I have written to you who believe in
the name of the Son of God, that you may know that
you have eternal life, and that you may continue to
believe in the name of the Son of God. (1 John 5:13)*

I know feelings shouldn't govern my life, but I like to
feel good. And as a dear friend once said to me, "It makes
you feel good, to feel good."

Some people expect a great rush of feelings when they
accept Christ as Savior. I remember only a feeling of relief
and peace when I invited Jesus into my heart.

Feelings are not always a dependable guide. Some days
I may not feel very Christlike. The confidence of my salvation rests in the Word of God. "But these are written that you

may believe that Jesus is the Christ, the Son of God, and that believing you may have life in His name" (John 20:31).

We are His children by faith because God says so. Our up and down feelings are not reliable. Christians do experience depression and discouragement. We still live in this flesh, even though we are indwelt by the Holy Spirit. What I need to remember when I "feel bad" is that God is still with me. His thoughts are for my good, and when I cry to Him for help, He *hears and answers,* according to His wisdom.

The Bible does not record that Job was told why all the calamities he suffered came upon him. Job did not curse or blame God, but when boils covered his body from his feet to his head Job became bitter and depressed. Job had a fleshly nature, too.

Feelings are fickle. Faith in God provides a firm foundation.

Prayer

When I don't "feel good," help me to remember not to be troubled and discouraged for You are with me always, Lord. In Your precious name I pray. Amen.

Learning Not to Fear

Even the darkness is not dark to Thee.
(Psalm 139:12 NASB)

When I was a child I was afraid of the dark. Even as a teenager I wanted someone with me when I was out at night. I remember a few times when I needed to walk four blocks home alone from our small town grocery store, where I worked on Friday nights. The familiar blocks became fraught with danger that lurked behind every bush and tree I passed. My heart pounded at the slightest noise. Fearing footsteps behind me, I ran the last two blocks not daring to look back. When I reached our front gate and with trembling hands lifted the latch, I sighed in relief. I could see lights inside my home and hear the murmur of my parents' voices. I was safe at home. The next day, as I walked the same blocks in sunshine, I knew my fears had been groundless.

There have been many similar nights in my life since then. I've grown in the knowledge of the One to whom darkness and light are alike. He took away my fears when I first had to be alone at night without my husband by my side. I prayed, "Lord, help me safely through the night." And He has. I can't say I really like being alone always, but there is peace and assurance in knowing that He who watches over me never sleeps.

There have been dark times of illness and sorrow when I remembered the words of the psalmist: "Whenever I am afraid, I will trust in You" (Ps. 56:3).

I do not choose to walk in darkness or purposely go out at night alone where there is possible danger. That would be foolish. But so are my fears when I know God has chosen the path I must walk. He knows where I am and why He has put me there.

Ahead of me is the "land of endless day." So I'll let His perfect love cast out my fears now until the day I'll be safe at home.

Prayer

How good to know that You are with me always, in darkness and in light. Forgive and take away all fears that try and keep me from walking by faith. In Jesus' name. Amen.

Learning in This Changing World

*But You are the same, and Your years will
have no end. (Psalm 102:27)*

"Oh, no," I protested as the morning paper announced the closing of a local department store.

That store had been in business as long as I could remember. So had a hardware store and drugstore that had closed recently. The new stores that had opened in their places did not carry the familiar merchandise of the old ones. I even liked the clutter of the old drugstore whose owner knew where everything could be found. The clerks in the new stores do not call me by name as the old ones did. I was having trouble adjusting to the changes.

"Nothing is sure but death and taxes," my father would tell me when I protested some change.

I can see, as I grow older, that I cannot expect things to remain the same. When I made a trip to the town in which I grew up, I found that the old church had been struck by lightning and had burned down. The new one doesn't have the old bell tower that called us to worship. The schoolhouse, my old home, and many other buildings were gone, and new ones had been built. Even the little creek that flowed by the edge of town was different and quite polluted.

"But the gospel that I first heard in that white frame church hasn't changed," I reassured myself. "Its truth is still the same."

Although the world around me keeps changing, as does my life, I am comforted by the One who never changes and promises to be with me always. Much in me needs changing and, as I yield to His will, He will change me to be more like Him. But He remains the same. Some day death will be no more—and I do not read of taxes in heaven—but "Jesus Christ is the same yesterday, today, and forever" (Heb. 13:8).

Prayer

Father, I thank You for Your unchanging love and mercy.
In this changing world, You are my rock and anchor,
the One who never fails me. Keep my eyes focused on You.
In Your Son's name. Amen.

Learning About Hospitality

Be hospitable to one another without grumbling.
(1 Peter 4:9)

I had been adjusting to living alone after my youngest son was married three and a half years ago. Gradually I began to develop a new routine for housework and meals. But there were lonely times. So when my son and his wife, with their eighteen-month-old son, needed a place to stay while their new home was being built, I invited them to stay with me. To my delight, they accepted.

The next four months were far from lonely. They were full of activity, laughter, and conversation. My daily routine went through another change.

My house was not always in order. Meals for four required more than a simple tray by the television. Phone and laundry times were shared. My daughter-in-law and I took turns preparing food. My son mowed the lawn and helped in other ways. I entertained my grandson, and he entertained us and kept us busy.

What a joy to hear his "dere's nama!" in the morning; to receive hugs and kisses from him morning and night. I enjoyed reading to him and listening to his chatter as he played.

And we were all learning each other's ways. We had promised to discuss any problems that arose. And we did. My children were considerate. I wanted to be the same.

The four months came to a close, and they moved into their new home. I put my house back in order, took my tray into the living room at mealtime, and was lonely.

I missed toys on the floor, shared meals and conversation, company at night, and not being alone. It was time to invite friends over, to have family dinners. I opened my home for a Bible study.

A home is for sharing.

Prayer

Lord, all that I have comes from You. Let my home always hold a welcome for others and reflect Your love. In Jesus' name. Amen.

Learning to Speak Wisely

The heart of the wise teaches his mouth, and adds
learning to his lips. (Proverbs 16:23)

The other night I watched the old Disney movie, *Bambi*. It was my way to relax after a stressful day.

One of my favorite scenes comes early in the movie. The forest animals are gathered to see the new prince, little Bambi, the deer. His mother coaxes Bambi to stand and greet his admirers. Bambi tries but his legs are very unsteady.

"Kinda wobbly, isn't he?" comments the little rabbit, Thumper.

"Thumper," admonishes his mother, "what did your father tell you this morning?"

In his best imitation of his father's stern voice, Thumper says, "If you can't say something nice, don't say nothing at all."

Little Thumper had a wise father.

I remember wise advice from my father.

"Words never spoken in anger do not have to be regretted."

Being "swift to hear, slow to speak, slow to wrath," are words I need to remember daily. My father's advice was good, as was that of little Thumper's father.

My husband was a quiet man who thought before he spoke. He had many friends. Most people enjoy the company of those who do not speak evil of others, who prefer to encourage and don't interrupt other people's conversations. People who show good manners and wisdom in speaking are good company.

Pleasant words are like a honeycomb, sweetness to the soul and health to the bones. (Proverbs 16:24)

Prayer

Lord, You have promised wisdom to all who ask in faith. Give me wisdom to speak only words that are wholesome. In Jesus' name I ask. Amen.

Learning What Is Necessary

*But one thing is needed, and Mary has chosen
that good part, which will not be taken
away from her. (Luke 10:42)*

I cleaned three shelves of a corner cupboard early this morning. I do my best work in the morning, it seems. I wake up full of energy and prefer working for an hour before eating breakfast. When my husband and sons were at home, I fixed breakfast and lunch boxes first. Now that I'm alone I often do many tasks first, then eat.

As I piled up a stack of papers, old booklets, and other outdated material, I sorted them into two piles. The "discard pile" proved to be higher than the "save pile." A lot of unnecessary paper went to the trash.

I thought about the day ahead of me.

"Lord," I prayed, "help me remove the unnecessary things from my schedule today. Give me wisdom to give my attention to what is truly necessary."

The day turned out quite differently from the way I had planned. I spent some time on the phone listening to a friend who needed a sympathetic ear. I decided to call on a neighbor I had been wanting to visit. The food committee on which I serve at church called for a meal to be delivered to a family whose mother was ill.

I still had more cupboards and drawers to clean. They were waiting but they hadn't had priority today, and I was satisfied that God had answered my prayer and given me more important tasks. The cupboards and drawers would wait.

I also examined myself and discarded some old resentments I found that had cluttered my mind for too long.

Getting rid of useless things leaves me with a good feeling. Ridding myself of sinful feelings makes me feel even better.

Prayer

Father, give me wisdom to know what is necessary each day.
Keep me from hoarding bad habits and sinful thoughts.
In Christ's name. Amen.

Learning Denial

"If anyone desires to come after Me, let him deny himself, and take up his cross, and follow Me."
(Matthew 16:24)

One lesson that it seems the Lord must teach me over and over again is that I must deny myself and live for Him. But I am learning. Obedience is coming more easily to me.

MISTAKEN IDENTITY

I called it insecurity,
God called it jealousy.
I said, "I'm better off alone."
God said, "Encourage those who are My own."

I was afraid to tell
of God's salvation free.

Jesus said, "You can't unless
you abide in Me."

"Help me, dear Lord," I finally cried.
And He did, as at last to self I died.
I died to self?
I thought I had.

But I had forgotten
The words of our Lord.
"If anyone wishes to follow Me,
He must deny himself daily."

I died to self?
Each day I live
if I would follow in
the steps of my Lord.

I must deny myself daily. Daily. Daily.

Prayer

Lord, help me to daily deny myself and follow You.
In Jesus' name. Amen.

Learning When a Father Dies

For whom the LORD loves He corrects;
just as a father the son in whom he delights.
(Proverbs 3:12)

Many times I have recalled my father's words since his death. I didn't always acknowledge their wisdom. I'm sorry, for now I do.

Dad had been given a small Bible when he was in his teens. He worked for the man who gave it to him and respected him. The Bible was precious to him, and he read it. He especially liked the book of Proverbs and said, "Their words help us live right."

Dad's mother had died when Dad was four, and his maternal grandmother raised him. He started working on farms at age twelve. He left school halfway through the tenth grade. He regretted this later and saw that we children completed our schooling. Never rich in worldly goods, he worked hard to provide for his wife and three children.

He loved us, talked to us, listened to us, laughed and joked with us—and he disciplined us. I didn't appreciate the last at the time.

"I love you," he'd say. "I only spanked you for your own good."

The book of Proverbs backed him up on this.

He did love us. When I would leave after a visit when he was older, he'd say, "I love you." He'd say it at the end of a telephone call, too. I knew he meant it.

The phone rang at 2:30 A.M., September 20, 1992. Before I answered, I knew what the message would be. My youngest son and I hurried to the nursing home. In the five minutes between nurses' checks, he had passed away.

"From earth to heaven," I said, "just as he wanted to go."

I looked at him lying there. I saw peace on his ninety-one-year-old face, which somehow looked younger.

"I love you, too, Dad," I whispered. I only wish I had said it more often.

Prayer

Thank You, heavenly Father, for fathers who correct us in love.
Even as You correct us in love for our good.
In Jesus' name. Amen.

Learning to Wait Again

Wait on the LORD; be of good courage, and He shall strengthen your heart; wait, I say, on the LORD!
(Psalm 27:14)

Cars were lined up for several blocks as the long freight train rumbled down the tracks. Once the final boxcar passed the intersection, the crossing arms slowly rose, and cars began to move over the tracks. But what was this! The crossing lights were red again, the warning signal was jingling and the crossing arms slowly descending.

I had moved up in line by possibly six cars. I wondered if there was a malfunction in the warning system. Then I saw, on the second set of tracks, the engine of a train coming from the opposite direction. Its long, drawn out whistle sounded as it approached. All we could do was *wait*.

Instead of fretting, I smiled as I indifferently observed the names on the cars whizzing by. I wasn't in a hurry. The plant fair I planned to attend was a short way across the tracks. My morning had been without the rush I usually experienced when I planned to do more than time allowed. Also, God had been teaching me lessons on waiting for many years. I've been a slow learner. I've never liked waiting for anything or anyone. And usually that was quite apparent to all around me.

So, how did the Lord teach me to wait patiently? By putting me in more and more situations where waiting was necessary. It also seemed He kept bringing Bible verses to my attention that called for waiting.

"I hate waiting, Father," I'd protest.

"Be still and know that I am God," His Word reminded me.

So I learned, by waiting, that He is in control and knows when I need to wait. As I waited now, I prayed. There are always things to pray about. I also thank Him for teaching me that waiting can be useful—when He is teaching me to *wait*.

Prayer

When You say wait, Father, help me to do it patiently,
with faith, realizing this is part of Your plan for my life.
In Jesus' name. Amen.

Learning Concern for Others

For I have no one like-minded, who will sincerely care for your state. (Philippians 2:20)

"I'm sorry, Aaron," said my son to his two-and-a-half-year-old son. "I can't wrestle with you tonight. My back hurts too much."

With grave concern, small Aaron knelt down on the rug where his father lay, trying to see his "hurting back."

"Too bad!" he said, shaking his head, "Get a Band-Aid."

"Thank you, Aaron," said his father, "I appreciate your sympathy."

We may not always have the right answer to another's hurts or problems (little Aaron didn't), but we can show we care. To Aaron a Band-Aid was a great help to cover hurts. As he grows older, he will learn, as we all do, that pain cannot always be eased with a simple Band-Aid covering.

But the sympathy we receive when we are suffering does help, in its own way. What if no one cared when we were hurting or sad or lonely? One of my favorite old hymns begins: "Somebody cares when you're lonely, tired, dejected, and blue," and closes, "that Someone is Jesus."

Yes, Jesus cares when we sorrow or suffer. He "comforts us so we may be able to comfort others." When a widow hugs another widow and says, "I know it's hard," there is an empathy that comes only when one has experienced the same sorrow. A parent who has lost a child can comfort someone presently facing this loss with real understanding.

It's good to know that the indwelling Holy Spirit enables us to love others as Christ loved us. With His help, we rejoice, empathize, and relate to others.

Prayer

Help me, Father, always to put others before myself and love them as You love me. In Jesus' name. Amen.

Learning from Wise Counsel

Listen to counsel and receive instruction, that you may be wise in your latter days. (Proverbs 19:20)

I should have gone straight ahead, but I turned left. We had hiked up the trail a few hours before, but I hadn't been very observant. Now, coming back, I had walked ahead of my son and daughter-in-law. I knew they would catch up with me. Orion, their golden retriever, walked beside me. On we went, but no one was overtaking us.

"Orion," I said, "do you suppose we are on the right trail?"

In answer Orion bounded ahead. I followed, still doubtful. Suddenly I heard a voice behind me.

"Where are you going, Mom?" the voice teased. I turned and saw my son.

"I took the wrong turn, didn't I? I wasn't sure."

"When in doubt, Mom, stand still and wait," my son gently rebuked. Tears of self-pity and weariness welled up in my eyes as we retraced my steps, uphill this time.

"Orion turned this way, and I thought he'd know." (When caught in a mistake, find someone to blame, even a dog.)

My son laughed, "Well, he was wrong, too. We're only eleven minutes on this trail. We'll rest whenever you want."

"No, I want to get back." Boy, was I feeling miserable.

My attitude didn't improve quickly. I was feeling ashamed even though my son was being considerate. When finally the Spirit took control instead of the flesh, I apologized for my attitude.

"When in doubt, wait," my son had said. Good advice.

Those who wait on the LORD shall renew
their strength. (Isaiah 40:31)

The one who waits on the Lord for direction won't take the wrong trail.

Prayer

Going my way often leads me in the wrong direction. Lord,
I should let You direct my steps. In Christ's name. Amen.

Learning from a Child

In everything give thanks; for this is the
will of God in Christ Jesus for you.
(1 Thessalonians 5:18)

The bottom dresser drawer holding the children's story books was stuck. Something was obviously obstructing its movement.

Three-year-old Aaron played beside me, only half concerned at my struggles.

I managed to open the drawer slightly, and I tried pushing a ruler through the small opening to find the offending obstacle.

It was no use.

"I'd better ask God for help, Aaron," I said. And I did.

Then I removed the drawer above the stuck one. A board remained, separating the two drawers, but somehow I was able to put my hand in and move a book lodged against the top of the drawer. The drawer opened easily, and Aaron joined me to take out his favorite books.

"Thank You, God," I murmured.

"God says you're welcome," Aaron replied.

His serious, natural response brought a smile to my face and made me think. I was pleased Aaron's parents were teaching him to be polite. Naturally, he believed God was polite, too. And wasn't He? Our Father in heaven, who instructs us to be thankful, is our perfect example.

I had never thought about God replying to my thanks but, from now on, I'm sure I will. God is willing to give. He tells us to ask with thanksgiving. Jesus healed ten lepers. When only one returned to thank Him, He asked, "Where are the other nine?"

Sometimes we feel unappreciated when we are not thanked for helping others. I don't believe God is like that. He keeps giving, to the grateful and ungrateful alike. But for our sake, He wants us to be thankful.

Prayer

Thank You, God, for receiving our thanks.
Thank You for Your love that gives and gives.
In Jesus' name. Amen.

Learning When a Mother Dies

*Listen to your father who begot you, and do not despise
your mother when she is old. (Proverbs 23:22)*

One o'clock P.M. and time to go to the nursing home to
see Mother. No, not anymore.

But in my thoughts I go. I see her hand reaching out to
me as I enter her room and, "June, June," she says, as she
shares something that is bothering her. I listen and assure
her that everything is all right.

It hasn't been quite two years since we took her to the
home to be with Dad. He had only been there a month. It
was good for them to be together. I went to visit with them
almost every day.

Then Dad passed away, and I kept going. Mother loved

to go out for rides and sometimes for lunch, too. During the summer, we made almost daily trips to the Dairy Queen down the street for her dish of ice cream. The employees there soon knew us. I would push her wheelchair around the block. "It feels good to be outside," she'd say. We talked. She missed her home and Dad. I often cried as I left. I wished she were able to be in her home, too.

Her life had changed. She had become weaker. She didn't have the desire to live without Dad. Many days, her thoughts went back to her childhood, and she wanted to see her "Mama" and "Papa."

She rallied after a bout with pneumonia. Then suddenly she became worse. In less than forty-eight hours, she took her last breath. And Mother had left us.

I miss her. I cry. I remember the many things she did for me and taught me. She is gone and now my life has changed.

Prayer

O Thou, who never changes, strengthen, comfort, and help me to adjust to another change in my life. Thank You for Your unchanging love. In Christ. Amen.

Learning to Keep Promises

Not a word failed of any good thing which
the LORD had spoken to the house of Israel.
All came to pass. (Joshua 21:45)

Resolution, January 1: "I resolve to lose ten pounds in two months."

Oh, how easy to make resolutions! How hard to keep them!

A new year seemed to inspire a fresh start. As I put up the new calendar I saw a clean page, unmarked as yet by appointments and other helpful reminders. It led me to make promises to myself (although the promise to diet had been encouraged by an earlier stand on the scales). A new year simply gave impetus to my resolution.

Time would tell, as the days of the calendar were marked off, whether I would succeed in keeping my promise. I had made it before, losing a few pounds, succumbing to old eating habits, and regaining them again.

With shame, I remembered other promises made recently and not carried out.

"I'll be sure to visit you soon."

"I'll pray for you."

"We'll have lunch together. I'll call you."

Well, I could do something about these promises now, and I would. I knelt and prayed for my friend. I called the other friend and made a lunch date. The lady I had promised to visit was surprised and delighted when I rang her doorbell later that day. I felt joy in finally keeping my promises. I also asked God to help me in the future not to be swift to make promises and slow to keep them.

God's promises are sure. He never forgets. He is faithful. How thankful I am for this assurance.

Prayer

Father, thank You for Your precious promises. I claim them by faith and ask You to help me to be faithful in all I do and say. In Jesus' name. Amen.

Learning from Memorizing

Your word I have hidden in my heart, that I might not sin against You. (Psalm 119:11)

I set my alarm for the early hour I had to rise in the morning. Then I settled down, hoping to go to sleep quickly. Not so. The mind is not easily turned off.

Okay. Time to use my tried and true method for falling asleep. Using the alphabet, I would begin to think through from *A* to *Z* on some topic. Maybe birds, flowers, countries of the world, cities, rivers, Bible names, and so forth. I usually don't reach the end of the alphabet before falling asleep.

What subject should I choose tonight? I decided to go in reverse and start at *Z*, naming things that had been part of my life since childhood. *Z*—zoo, always fun to go there; *Y*—Yo-yos, had fun learning to do tricks with those; *X*—

xylophone, I played one in grammar school. To my amazement, I was remembering a tune I played. The hammer hit the keys, "g a g c g a g." I hadn't played that tune in fifty-five years. How did I remember it? Was it true that all we've learned is stored in our mind?

I finally dropped off to sleep, but the next morning the old tune returned to my mind, and I hummed it over and over.

I remember hearing of prisoners during the Korean War who shared Bible verses through their walls in prison. In one cell, a prisoner would begin a verse, and in the next cell, another would finish it. Verses they had memorized, perhaps even as children, came to mind to comfort and encourage them.

A missionary friend once said, "What if our Bible was taken away from us? It's happened in other countries."

So I began to memorize Bible verses. They have helped me again and again, just when I needed their wisdom and encouragement most.

Memorizing and obeying keeps God's Word in our hearts.

Prayer

Thank You, dear God, for Your Word that teaches, reproves, corrects, and trains us in righteousness. In Jesus' name. Amen.

Learning How Near God Is

*And lo, I am with you always, even to the end
of the age. Amen. (Matthew 28:20)*

"Be with Mary in her grief," prayed the man.

Inwardly I sighed. Not that I wasn't agreeing that Mary needed God's presence. I was. But Mary was a Christian, and Christians have God's promise that He is always with us.

Perhaps I was becoming overly critical of this prayer. I had heard it so often. After all, it is the meaning of the prayer, not the words themselves, that matters. Still, the assurance of God's ever-abiding presence had become more certain for me lately. I wondered why Christians would ask God to be with them when He had already said He was. His Holy Spirit indwells the believer.

Moses reminded the Israelites of God's promise when they seemed to have forgotten it: "And the LORD, He is the one who goes before you. He will be with you, He will not leave you nor forsake you; do not fear nor be dismayed" (Deut. 31:8).

Perhaps what is really meant when we pray for God to be with someone is that they may find strength and guidance from His abiding presence. His presence is all the help we need. David speaks often in the psalms of this help. In Psalm 46 he says, "God is our refuge and strength, a very *present* help in trouble" (v. 1, emphasis added).

Someone once said, "What a comfort it would be to know, when we are praying, that Christ was in the next room praying for us."

He is nearer than that.

Prayer

Thank You, eternal Father, that You are with me always. For without You, I can do nothing. In Christ's name. Amen.

Learning True Comfort

*The eternal God is your refuge, and underneath are
the everlasting arms. (Deuteronomy 33:27)*

In my morning quiet time, I was reading a devotional
written by a father. He had written about his one-year-old
son's morning. First, the baby had wanted up; next he didn't
want out of his bath. Then his diaper was messy, and he cried
until he was changed. When fed, he fussed over his food.
Put on the floor to play, he fussed some more. He was all
smiles as they carried him back to bed with his bottle. But
in a few minutes he was crying again. What did he want?

As I read, it seemed to me that all the baby wanted was
to be held and given attention. Only then would he be happy.

I sympathized. There are times when nothing satisfies
me. I need to be held in love and given attention. At such
times, my only comfort comes from drawing near to God

in the only way I can. I pray and read His Word. I rest in His promises. I know God is listening to my prayers. "Evening and morning and at noon I will pray, and cry aloud, and He shall hear my voice" (Ps. 55:17).

I do not understand how God is everywhere, hears every prayer, loves each one of us individually, and knows everything about us. I only know He says He does, and I believe and am comforted.

I can't stay all day letting Him hold me (although He's always near). He lifts me gently to my feet and sends me to comfort and serve others, in His love.

What has happened to change my unhappy outlook?

I've rested awhile, figuratively, in God's arms, and I've found strength and help for the day. All I needed was some comforting.

Prayer

God of all comfort, I thank You that You know my needs.
Let me remember that I am comforted so I can comfort others.
In Jesus' name. Amen.

Learning About Homes

*And Jesus said to him, "Foxes have holes
and birds of the air have nests, but the Son of Man
has nowhere to lay His head." (Matthew 8:20)*

The robin flew from the low evergreen as I mowed my lawn. Curious, I stopped the mower and peered into the branches of the bush. Almost hidden was a small nest with four tiny blue eggs in it.

"Oh, so that's it!" I exclaimed. "I'm getting too close to Mrs. Robin's home."

I was careful after that only to look in the nest when I was sure mother robin was away from it. She was never far away, though. I could hear her scolding chirp. Several weeks later, when I looked in the bush I saw what seemed like a bit of brown fluff. The baby birds were hatching. Soon there were four tiny balls of feathers, squirming and opening yellow bills for food. Gradually, orange spots of color appeared on the tiny bodies. My grandchildren had joined me in peeks at the nest. They were delighted to watch a robin family grow. I was glad the robin had decided my bush was a safe place for her nest.

I had a house finch make her nest in my hanging plant outside the kitchen window last summer. And when our sons were young, sparrows made a nest inside a cover that had come loose from the window air conditioner. We had a good view of this sparrow family. Yes, birds make nests in strange places.

God sent His own Son to dwell on earth. But Jesus did not establish a home of His own here. We do, and when God is our head and is the One we trust and obey, we have a safe place to raise our families. We can be assured, too, that, when our time on earth is finished, God will have a heavenly home prepared for us.

Prayer

*Thank You, Father, for homes. Thank You for Your daily care.
Keep us ever abiding in You. In Jesus' name. Amen.*

Learning to Seek Shelter

For You have been a shelter for me, and a strong tower from the enemy. (Psalm 61:3)

Storm warning: Snow continuing through the day and night, accumulation of eight to ten inches expected.

I sat at my window watching the tiny flakes pile up on everything outside. Warmly dressed, I had earlier replenished my bird feeders. Now I watched as black-capped chickadees, cardinals, blue jays, sparrows, phoebes, and downy woodpeckers darted from the branches of the spruce and pecked away at the bird food and suet. I could see them flitting from limb to limb in the tree between feedings. The tree was their shelter from the storm.

My physical shelter was inside my house. There, cozy and warm, I could enjoy watching the world rapidly turning white.

Birds, beasts, and people—we all seek shelter in a storm. But life has many different kinds of storms. Some need more than physical shelter. In that kind of storm, the Bible says we have a shelter in God.

A friend and I were talking by phone of the trials and testings of the past year. It had been a particularly difficult year for us both, with sickness in her family and the death of a parent in mine.

"I don't know," she said, "how I would have kept on without the assurance of God's help."

I agreed.

A flock of starlings swooped down and began feeding. Then suddenly, as if startled, they rose up and flew away. I can't always see what alarms the birds but, whatever it is, it sends them flying to shelter. Often it is the unseen and unknown that sends me fearfully to the Lord, and I wait upon Him, remembering His promise, "I will never leave you nor forsake you" (Heb. 13:5).

Prayer

Thank You, heavenly Father, for being our eternal refuge. Your perfect love casts out fear and calms us as we seek shelter in You. In Jesus' name. Amen.

Learning by Imitation

The things which you learned
and received and heard and saw in me, these do.
(Philippians 4:9)

His daddy was mowing my lawn. He followed behind, pushing his small toy lawn mower, turning when his daddy turned, and stopping when he stopped. When they finished, he pushed his mower to the truck and put it in with his daddy's. As they sat down to visit, I smiled as little legs crossed and arms folded across his chest, an exact replica of his daddy beside him.

"I better do things right, hadn't I?" said the daddy as he noticed me observing his son's actions.

"Yes," I agreed. "You have someone copying you."

I remember how our three sons followed their father as

he did repairs around the house and on the car. They were learning to do things the way their dad did, even then.

Today, as I shelled the peas I had picked earlier in the cool of the day, I thought of the many times I had sat by my father, shelling peas and talking. He really enjoyed shelling peas. Could that be why I enjoy what many find a tiring chore? Dad made shelling peas a pleasant task.

I know I do many things the way my parents did. I remember hearing a story (whether true or not, I do not know) of a mother who cut the bone from her ham before putting it on to cook. When her daughter asked why, she said, "Because my mother did." The daughter then asked the grandmother why she had removed the bone, and the grandmother said, "Because my mother did." Undaunted, the daughter visited the frail great-grandmother, now in a nursing home, and asked her the same question. "So it would fit in my pan," explained the great-grandmother simply.

Christ is our perfect example.

Prayer

Help me, Father, to keep my eyes on Jesus, the author and perfecter of my faith, and to follow Him. In His name. Amen.

Learning How God Sees

"For the LORD does not see as man sees; for man looks at the outward appearance, but the LORD looks at the heart." (1 Samuel 16:7)

"I love to fix my family a meal appropriate to the holiday," an acquaintance once told me. "But I certainly made a mistake one St. Patrick's Day," she giggled.

"What did you fix?" I asked.

"Well, I had forgotten about the day until I was fixing our evening meal. The only green thing I had was a jar of pickles, which wouldn't be unusual. I thought of cutting my meat loaf into shamrock-shaped slices but decided that might be a little far-fetched. So . . ." She broke into peals of laughter again.

"So what?" I demanded.

"So I put green food coloring in my mashed potatoes."

I gasped. The picture I envisioned of green mashed potatoes was not appealing.

"Did they eat them?"

"At first they just looked at them, and Billy said, 'Mom, they don't look very good.' I guess it's true that we eat with our eyes, too."

I don't remember how she said the potatoes tasted, and I've never tried to find out. A dish of fluffy white mashed potatoes, dripping with butter, looks so appetizing. Why should I spoil it?

It's easy to cover skin flaws with makeup and enhance our appearance with pretty clothes and an attractive hairstyle, but a Christian's outward appearance starts from the inside, in the heart. We can deceive others, but we can't deceive God. He looks at our heart.

I'd rather be good than look good.

Prayer

Because You know me truly, Father, I can trust You
to correct me and guide me in the right way.
Thank You, in Jesus' name. Amen.

Learning to Change Plans

Cause me to hear Your lovingkindness in the morning,
for in You do I trust; cause me to know the way in
which I should walk, for I lift up my soul to You.
(Psalm 143:8)

I awakened to the sound of raindrops on the roof and window pane. Before I had dropped off into a sound sleep, I remembered seeing flashes of lightning and hearing the sound of muffled thunder. It must have rained all night.

Well, that changed my plans for the day. I had planned to work outside, trimming a bush and weeding a particularly unsightly spot in my backyard. But I didn't mind the change. It wasn't the first time weather had changed my plans. One thing I have learned in my accumulating years is that work usually waits for you until another day.

Rainy-day plans began to form. I had been praying for

a less hectic schedule, for time to write and read. The Lord answered with a rainy day. It was up to me to use it wisely. I could spend a little more time in the Word and in prayer this morning. I needed that.

Maybe, I thought, getting older makes you more accepting of changes. Then I remembered. A few weeks ago, I complained exceedingly about a change in a trip I was planning. I had prayed that, if God did not want me to travel alone, He would provide companionship, and He did. But I still felt I wanted to go alone. Gently and firmly, I knew God was directing. Best of all, He helped with my attitude as I yielded to His will. I began to look forward to my friend's companionship on the trip.

Even as I grow older, I still must be reminded that asking God to direct my ways means willingly to accept His direction and the changes He makes.

No murmuring and complaining!

Prayer

You know I've always had trouble accepting changes, Father.
Help me to accept changes in my life willingly and
with thankfulness, for Your wisdom lies behind them.
In Jesus' name. Amen.

Learning from Repetition

Finally, my brethren, rejoice in the Lord.
For me to write the same things to you is not tedious,
but for you it is safe. (Philippians 3:1)

"Tell me what this is again."

I smiled and turned to look at the tool my three-and-a-half-year-old grandson had pulled out of a box of things his grandpa had saved.

"I don't know what it is. I'm sorry," I said. "Grandpa must have been saving it for some reason."

I had told him this before. He wasn't satisfied with my repetitious answer but if I said I didn't know, well, I didn't. Maybe someday we'd both find out what he wanted to know by showing the tool to someone who knew what it was.

But I wish I knew now! I wish I had the answers to a lot

of things. Many things in my life have caused me to question God again!

"What is the purpose of this trial I'm going through, Father? Will you please tell me?"

The answer is always in His Word (again).

> *Knowing that the trying of your faith*
> *produces patience. (James 1:3)*
>
> *Now no chastening seems to be joyful for the present*
> *but grievous; nevertheless, afterward it yields the*
> *peaceable fruit of righteousness to those who have been*
> *trained by it. (Hebrews 12:11)*

"What is this?" my grandson asks, holding out a rusty piece of metal.

"Oh, that's an old saw blade," I answer. "Too rusty to be any good."

"Too rusty," he repeats putting it down, satisfied because he has an answer.

Sometimes when I ask God "Why?" the answer comes quickly.

Sooner or later, He always has the right answer.

Prayer

Thank You, Lord, that You are willing to instruct me over
and over again until I finally learn to trust and obey.
In Jesus' name. Amen.

Learning As Time Passes

"This is My body which is given for you; do this
in remembrance of Me." (Luke 22:19)

"This would have been our golden anniversary."

I nodded sympathetically. My friend had been widowed only a few months. She would learn, as I had, that birthdays, anniversaries, holidays, and any other special days would be difficult without the one who had shared them before.

I remember how hard it was when our wedding anniversary date arrived two months after my husband's death. Then came our oldest son's birthday, Thanksgiving, and Christmas. Each was made more poignant by the "empty chair."

Time ticks on. It is somewhat easier now, after a number of years, to reminisce.

"Remember the Christmas Dad and I both received a gas saw?" our oldest son asks.

"Dad would have this put together in no time," says our youngest son, struggling with an unassembled present.

I smile at their memories while my heart feels a moment's pang. We miss our husband and father, but we can remember him more easily now.

Choosing to remain in our home made me face decisions my husband had always made. When I wasn't sure of what to do, I prayed. God is faithful. He sent the help and guidance I needed, time after time. Sometimes I would remember my husband's instructions about something baffling me, and I'd know what to do.

Jesus knew it would be difficult for His disciples when He left them, so He told them, "Remember the word that I said to you" (John 15:20).

Prayer

Lord, You have promised to be with us always. You know when we feel inadequate, unable to cope, and in need of Your guidance and help. Thank You, Father. In Jesus' name. Amen.

Learning He Is Holding

Even there Your hand shall lead me, and Your right hand shall hold me. (Psalm 139:10)

The young mother leading her four children out the door of the church looked over at me and smiled.

"Isn't it precious to hold that little hand?" she asked.

I looked down at my three-year-old grandson, whose hand was securely in mine.

"Yes, it is." I smiled back at her.

It is infinitely precious to have a little one place his hand confidently in yours and walk along beside you. At the same time, you desire to be worthy of that trust, whether walking across a street or through a crowded store. You take an extra measure of caution as you hold onto that little hand.

Children learn to walk as hands are held out to them, encouraging them to keep trying.

There are times when I stumble and fall in my Christian walk. I need encouragement to rise again. There is greater love and security in the hands of our God reaching out to us and taking hold of us than we can ever fully comprehend.

Peter denied Jesus three times. Could he ever walk with Jesus again? Jesus asked Peter three times if he loved Him, and three times Jesus told Peter to "feed my sheep." Of His sheep, Jesus said, "My Father, who has given them to Me, is greater than all; and no one is able to snatch them out of My Father's hand" (John 10:29).

Our Father's hands are strong.

Prayer

Thank You, Lord, for holding me, setting me on my feet when I fall, and teaching me how to walk. In Jesus' precious name. Amen.

Learning During Storms

The clouds poured out water; the skies sent out
a sound; Your arrows also flashed about. The voice of
Your thunder was in the whirlwind; the lightnings lit
up the world; the earth trembled and shook.
(Psalm 77:17–18)

Going to close a window, I noticed a strange stillness in the air. A sudden gust of wind hit my face. Lightning flashed, thunder roared, and raindrops began to pound on the roof and windows.

I grabbed my transistor radio and flashlight and hurried to the basement stairway. There I sat, anxiously listening to an announcer's voice urging people to get to shelter. Already many streets were blocked by falling trees throughout the city. I sat and prayed. The lights blinked but remained on. When the storm finally waned, it was night. I could not discern all that had occurred outside. I could see the hackberry tree my husband had planted thirty-five years ago lying against the corner of the house. I could do nothing now. I went to bed.

The next morning I looked out at a scene of chaos. Branches and leaves covered the lawn. Across the street, my neighbors' sycamore tree was uprooted and lay across their roof. The next few weeks were busy as the work of cleaning up began throughout the city. The only damage to my roof was the eaves trough, which could be replaced. Later I would plant a new tree, too. But scars left from the storm remained for many months.

There are usually reminders left from the storms we face in life—some physical, some emotional, some mental. Storms of life can be endured more readily when we know God is with us. He is in control. He has a purpose for each storm.

"Be still," He says, "and know that I am God" (Ps. 46:10).

The God who causes storms also sends healing and renewing.

Storms pass. God is forever.

Prayer

Father, I'm glad to know You are with me in every storm.
Keep me ever close to You, and I will not fear.
In Jesus' name. Amen.

Learning from Others' Hospitality

Better is a dinner of herbs where love is, than a
stalled ox and hatred therewith. (Proverbs 15:17)

"Come for dinner and talking," the handmade invitation read.

Julia, one of the five-year-old twins, and Amos, the oldest of the seven children, had delivered the invitation to me.

Now, with nine other ladies, I was here at their farm home. We were all friends of the mother of the seven children and of their grandmother, who lived in her trailer home beside them. The father had gone hunting, and the mother had decided to entertain old friends. "Older in age," we were, too, and alone in our own homes.

It was such a special time. The children had made place

cards for the table. As we sat down, the mother had us share something about ourselves, and conversation blossomed. The children ate nicely, listening and joining in when addressed.

A few years ago, I had lunched in a log cabin in the wilderness. The man who lived there year round had served cold sourdough pancakes spread with peanut butter and honey, blueberries with powdered milk, and hot tea. I thought at that time I could not have enjoyed my meal more if it had been served on gold plates in a palace.

I felt that way now. Our table had been simply set. The delicious roast, potatoes, broccoli, and salads were passed around, along with the grandmother's homemade bread. Later on, we enjoyed cookies, coffee, and tea in the living room.

Love was there—love that practiced hospitality and taught sharing, love that came from God, who first loved us.

Hospitality blesses the one offfering it and the one receiving it.

Prayer

Lord, help me practice hospitality. Let the love which
You have shown me shine through all I do and say.
In Jesus' name. Amen.

Learning to Discard

That you put off, concerning your former conduct,
the old man which grows corrupt according to the
deceitful lusts. (Ephesians 4:22)

"If I haven't worn a dress in over five years, I give it away," my friend said.

Good idea! But I don't find it that easy to do. I reason to myself that there may be an occasion when I'll wish I had that dress.

As my closet becomes more crowded, my reasoning becomes weaker. Determinedly, I begin to sort and soon have a sizable bundle for our church's clothing outlet. I've also had to face up to having gained a few pounds the last few years.

Raised on the "wear-it-out" theory by a father who saved almost everything, I have always found it hard to discard. However, after closing the homes of my husband's parents and my own parents, I have seen the importance of letting go of what you are no longer using. Still, it's not an easy task. It takes determination and perseverance.

It seems as if I have the same problem with my old nature. It is still around even though I have been given a new nature from God. "Put off the old one," God's Word admonishes. Those old habits I've kept for so long do not fit in the new life I have in Christ. Gossip, grudges, envy, jealousy, pride, anger, and impatience must all be cast out. Then God will give me a "new heart of mercy, kindness, humility, gentleness, and patience."

When I give away old clothes I no longer need, hopefully someone else can use them. But my old habits and sins are to be discarded completely. They are of no good to anyone.

When my life isn't cluttered with old sinful habits, there is room for Christ to fill it and to work there.

What do I need to discard?

Prayer

Help me not to hold onto that which no longer fits into my walk with You, Father. In Jesus' name. Amen.

Learning to Rejoice in Trials

Rejoice in the Lord always. Again I will say, rejoice!
(Philippians 4:4)

"I was really having a hard time after my car accident finding something to rejoice about," my friend said. (I knew the feeling.)

But my friend went on.

"I got down on my knees and asked God to help me. After that, I sat down and, as I thought of people who had come to help me after the accident, I soon had a list of eighteen things for which to be thankful."

"I didn't feel like rejoicing as I sat in church," the daughter of another friend confessed. "My husband had left us and I had lots of expenses. Then I looked across the aisle and saw our evangelism pastor's young married daughter with a turban on her head. I knew she was having radiation after her brain tumor operation and I thought, all your children are well. I was ashamed that I'd felt I had nothing to rejoice about."

Sometimes it is difficult, almost impossible, to rejoice when trials fill our days. God did not say our days on earth would be trouble free. I guess some would say trials are as certain as death and taxes. I've also heard that, if everyone were to put their troubles into one huge basket and then choose one, people would take their own back. That could be true. Usually we can look around and see others with greater trials than our own. God knows how much we can bear.

We have a Savior who suffered for all in order to take the penalty for sin, which was death. We can rejoice in this always. He is also our burden bearer. "Casting all your care upon Him, for He cares for you" (1 Peter 5:7).

We can rejoice in the Lord, and He will guide us through our trials.

Prayer

Jesus, You suffered for sinners and said, "Not My will, but Yours, be done" (Luke 22:42). For this we rejoice always. In Your precious name. Amen.

Learning of Limited Sight

I will instruct you and teach you in the way
you should go; I will guide you with My eye.
(Psalm 32:8)

As I prepared to start up another hill, a sign beside the country road caught my eye. "Limited View Ahead," it read. The road was new to me so I believed the sign and slowed down. The hills I had been going up and down the last few miles were steep, and I often reached the top before I could see if another car was coming. As I started up this hill I saw another sign, indicating a driveway from an adjoining farm bordered by tall pine trees. There was, indeed, a need for alertness. I reached the top of the hill safely. I was glad the warning sign had made me more alert.

As I go through life I don't have any visible signs to tell me I have a limited view ahead. But I know it's true. I make plans and fill up my calendar with appointments and engagements. Sometimes I plan several months ahead. But, in all these plans, the Bible reminds me that I ought to say, "If the Lord wills, we shall live and do this or that" (James 4:15).

I've lived long enough to know my plans may be changed sometimes. When I was younger I would be disappointed, even angry, when plans were thwarted. Usually, I learned there were good reasons why everything did not go the way I planned or wished.

I realize that I may not always know immediately, or perhaps ever, the reasons for changed plans. I know that only God can see "over the hill." Proverbs 3:6 says, "In all your ways acknowledge Him, and He shall direct your paths."

I'm glad I have a guide who knows the way I should go and who promises to alert me to any possible dangers ahead.

My view is limited. God's isn't.

Prayer

I'm glad You know the way I should take every day, Father.
It's satisfying and exciting to let You guide me.
In Jesus' name. Amen.

Learning Trials Are Necessary

In this you greatly rejoice, though now for a little while, if need be, you have been grieved by various trials. (1 Peter 1:6)

Little did I know, as I rejoiced in a weak prayer answered this morning and as I shared the pain of another whose cancer had returned, that before the day was half over I would be facing a crisis in my own family.

How trivial our paltry discomforts, our minor disappointments, and our petty complaints seem at times like these. How humbly we bow before almighty God, confess our sins, and seek His mercy and guidance.

This morning our pastor had spoken on 1 Peter 1:6–9 (how we were to live and walk while we are being tested).

As I sat in the pew taking notes and receiving encouragement from God's Word, I knew from past experience how hard it is to be glad in the midst of trials. That I did learn to be glad was because I looked, not to what I could see, but to the One I could believe. The power of God, my salvation by faith, and my heavenly inheritance were my hope and consolation. I could only walk by faith in God knowing that He promises to be with me and guide me.

I was being tested again. Could I see God's answer in the prayers sent to His throne for a son and his wife? I knew that the more I became absorbed in this trial the larger it would become. God's Word says trials come (if necessary) to increase faith in Him. IF NECESSARY! Sometimes the only way God can bring us to Himself is to bring us to the place where we are completely powerless to "work things out."

Albert Einstein said, "Believing is seeing."

I do believe, and God's precious promises cause me to rejoice, knowing that nothing comes into the life of His children but by His will.

Not my will but Thine be done.

Prayer

Lord, I cannot see in this trial. It is hard even to rejoice. But because You say we are to "count it joy," I obey and trust Your guidance and will now. In Jesus' name. Amen.

Learning
How to Teach

Early in the morning He came again into
the temple, and all the people came to Him;
and He sat down and taught them. (John 8:2)

A good friend was tutoring neighbor Vietnamese children. They were new to our country and there was much to learn. The oldest girl came to my friend with a question from her school lesson.

"Which one doesn't belong; a knife, scissors, or a screwdriver?" she asked, obviously puzzled. "What is a screwdriver?"

My friend went to a drawer, brought out a screwdriver, and showed it to the girl.

"Oh, I see," she said, as a smile lit up her face. "The screwdriver doesn't belong. It isn't sharp."

I've found, when guiding women's Bible studies, that sometimes words Christians use readily are not that clear to those just beginning to study the Bible. So I try to use examples for many words, such as *born again, justification,* and even *sin.*

My four-year-old grandson quickly latches onto any new word we use when talking to him. He wants to know immediately what it means. Sometimes I have to think carefully for an example to explain the word.

Jesus did much of His teaching in parables. He knew the people would understand things they saw every day. Jesus said, "Look at the birds, they don't sow or reap but God feeds them." He used lilies, seeds, and sheep to help people understand God's love and how He wanted them to live. He demonstrated God's Word by His life.

I do not know what it would be like to move to a country where I needed to learn a new language. I think, as with my friend's Vietnamese neighbors, it would help if I were shown an example for words I did not understand.

Jesus explained God by His example.

Prayer

Father, give me understanding as I read Your Word. Help me to obey the things You teach me. In Jesus' name. Amen.

Learning to Walk at My Own Pace

I, therefore, the prisoner of the Lord, beseech you
to have a walk worthy of the calling with which
you were called. (Ephesians 4:1)

I truly enjoyed hiking wilderness trails with my son and daughter-in-law. But where they climbed with agility up the mountain trail, I stumbled. After one minor tumble that only bruised my pride, I ended up in a sitting position. My son turned around and teasingly said, "If you wanted to rest, Mom, you should have just told us."

I made a face at him and stood up, determined to keep my eyes on the trail.

When we finally reached the alpine meadow at the end

of the trail, I was glad I had persevered. A river flowed through the valley below.

A marmot's shrill whistle sounded from nearby rocks. We stretched out on the grass and let the sun warm us as we rested and ate our lunch. Going back down I sent them on ahead. "I know the way now," I told them, "let me walk at my own pace. I'll make it."

When I reached my children's cabin, they were busy at other tasks, but they took time to express pleasure at my effort.

"If I do as well as you have when I'm sixty-three," my daughter-in-law said, "I'll be glad."

I glowed under the unexpected praise.

Is my heavenly Father pleased with my walk, stumbling and slow as it is at times, I wondered.

The answer came to me that God is patient and always goes ahead. I wouldn't stumble as much if I followed His steps. If my pace is slow but steady and on the straight and narrow path, although I may stumble at times He'll be there to pick me up and set me back on the path.

Perseverance pays.

Prayer

Father, You know my pace may be slower than others.
Help me to keep my eyes on You and walk in Your steps.
In Your Son's name. Amen.

Learning in Silence

The LORD is in His holy temple. Let all the earth keep silence before Him. (Habakkuk 2:20)

Silence is golden! Quiet times are precious times to meditate on God's Word. This is easier when nothing else is demanding our attention.

This winter morning I arose early while it was still dark. A few bright stars shone near a crescent moon. There was no hum of traffic. There were no lights in nearby houses. All was still.

"I know that You are God," I whispered in prayer, "and You alone know what the day will bring. Guide and direct me in all my ways. Thank You for Your promises and love."

Before long, the sky brightened, lights shone from houses, and traffic began to move on the busy road a few blocks away. Birds came to the feeders for breakfast. I heard the thump of the morning paper against the front door. It was still quiet in my house except for the ticking of the clocks and the comforting sound of the furnace fan. So I read my Bible and prayed again.

By the time the telephone rang and I turned on my radio for news, I was ready for the noise and bustle of another day. Company came and the house was full of chatter and laughter. The only silent time was when heads were bowed for mealtime blessing.

Night came. Company gone. Quiet again! When we live alone silent times come more often. As I lay in bed, I could hear a dog barking far off. In the still of the night, I heard the whistle of a train a mile away. Then silence, comforting silence—God was awake.

"He who keeps you will not slumber" (Ps. 121:3). I closed my eyes and slept.

Prayer

Thank You for quiet times when I can draw near to You. They are golden times. Help me to treat them as such. In my Savior's name. Amen.

Learning About Recognition

"And he calls his own sheep by name. . . .
I am the good shepherd; and I know My sheep,
and am known by My own." (John 10:3, 14)

The evening church service was underway. I was seated with friends toward the rear of the church. Suddenly I heard a familiar voice call out clearly, "Hi, Nama." I turned my head to see my four-year-old grandson seated by his father, waving and smiling at me. All around us people were smiling and chuckling. I waved back and smiled. What else was a grandma to do! Obviously his father did some admonishing for there was no more talking from my grandson and, during the singing of the hymn preceding the sermon, he left to join the other children his age at their own "children's church."

Little children do not hesitate to recognize audibly those

they love, no matter where they are. They can be standing in front of an audience or riding in a grocery cart in a crowded supermarket. In fact, most anytime, anywhere, spotting the familiar face (or back) of one they love elicits an eager, happy greeting. And speaking for one grandma, "I love it."

Everywhere, anywhere, when people are called by name and see the loving, happy face of the familiar greeter, they feel pleasure in being recognized. But adults tend not to call out at inappropriate times.

Jesus said, "I know your name. I know you, and I love you." What greater joy could there be than to have our Savior call us by name?

If we are ashamed to acknowledge Him anytime, anywhere, it must grieve Him, but His love does not change. He waits for us to "grow in the grace and knowledge of our Lord and Savior Jesus Christ" (2 Peter 3:18). Surely, as we learn to know and love Him, we will not be ashamed to recognize Him anytime, anywhere.

Prayer

Lord, let me never be ashamed of acknowledging You and Your words. May my love for You grow day by day. In Jesus' name. Amen.

Learning to Bear One Another's Burdens

*Bear one another's burdens, and so fulfill
the law of Christ. (Galatians 6:2)*

"Hey, if you have a problem, we have a problem."

This was a father's response to a young daughter who was having trouble falling asleep in her tent on a family vacation. She crawled into her parents' tent, apologizing for being a problem, and the father quickly assured her of their concern.

Some days it seems as if half the people we talk to have problems.

With some, the problems are so great that our heart is troubled for them, and we earnestly seek for ways to help.

With others, though, the most we can do is pray, knowing we have a Burden Bearer who can always help.

Bearing another's burden may simply mean paying a visit and listening. I have a neighbor who doesn't move around well, and she appreciates company.

As I help sort clothes and bedding at our city's mission outlet, I am thankful for all who gave so that those in need could receive help. The young man in charge has great empathy for those who come in for help.

"I've been in their place," he says.

Jesus said to those who asked how they could serve Him, "if you have two coats, give to one who has none."

Once, after reading these words in Luke 3:11, I went to my closet and looked at the two good coats hanging there. One I scarcely wore anymore. So I took it to the mission for someone who had none.

Jesus doesn't want anyone to bear their burdens all alone. He is our burden bearer. He is also our example. When we follow Him we *will* bear burdens.

Love cares.

Prayer

Father, thank You that I don't have to bear my burdens alone.
And thank You that I can help share another's burden.
In Your Son's name. Amen.

Learning to Accept Advice

*Apply your heart to instruction, and your
ears to words of knowledge. (Proverbs 23:12)*

I'm learning to play golf.

I decided to learn a few years ago, after hearing it was a game you could play into your eighties and nineties if you were healthy enough. That sounded good.

I took some lessons but never actually played a game the first year. I only had two clubs. The next year became a real time of learning, as I acquired a few more clubs and a golf bag. Advice came from good golfers who were kind enough to play with me. I tried to follow their instructions but sometimes I felt confused, discouraged, and yes, sometimes I admit, resented their words.

I checked out a book on golf from the library. There I read how professional golfers taught others, and I realized they were giving the same instructions my friends had been giving me. I had been acting like a child who says, "I can do it myself," but ends up failing and asking for help. I had much to learn.

The book of Proverbs contains words of wisdom and instruction.

> *Hear instruction and be wise,*
> *and do not disdain it. (8:33)*
>
> *Give instruction to a wise man,*
> *and he will be still wiser. (9:9)*

The children of Israel did not follow God's instructions when they tried to gather manna in the wilderness on the Sabbath. They found none. And when they saved some from other days until the next morning, it bred worms and became foul. They learned by their mistakes.

We can learn from our mistakes, but we could learn faster if we would only follow the instructions given by those with knowledge.

God says, "Listen and obey."

Prayer

I've tried to do things my way, Lord, instead of asking for Your guidance and listening to wise counsel. Thank You for showing me I was wrong. Help me to be teachable. In Jesus' name. Amen.

Learning to Bear Fruit

You will know them by their fruits. Do men gather
grapes from thornbushes or figs from thistles?
(Matthew 7:16)

The car pulled out from a side road in front of me, then proceeded slowly.

"C'mon," I grumbled, " Let's go faster than ten miles an hour."

My impatience increased as the car continued to go its slow rate. Ahead I could see a red light at the intersection.

"Well," I reasoned, "maybe he's going slow so the light will be green when he reaches it."

I've done that sometimes so I didn't have to come to a full stop.

The light changed to green, and he increased his speed

slightly. Thankfully, he went straight, and I managed to make my left turn under an amber light, changing to red.

Still inwardly fuming, I was beginning to feel conviction.

"That wasn't exactly patience or self-control you were showing," I told myself. No, it wasn't.

I once heard an older Christian lady say, "When you see good in me, it's the Holy Spirit working. The bad is my old self showing through."

It seems I can see how others could be more patient and self-controlled. But the real test of my obedience to the Holy Spirit is when someone or something is irritating me. Jesus said there was no reward in loving those who loved you or doing good to people who treat you well. God is kind to the ungrateful and evil. We, who are His, should be reflecting His love.

The fruit of the Spirit is love, joy, peace, long-suffering, kindness, goodness, faithfulness, gentleness, self-control. (Galatians 5:22–23)

Prayer

Help me to walk according to the Spirit and bear good fruit. In Jesus' name. Amen.

Learning As Spring Comes Again

For lo, the winter is past, the rain is over and gone.
The flowers appear on the earth; the time of singing
has come. (Song of Solomon 2:11–12)

Mornings are filled with bird songs again. Crocuses pop up in forgotten spots. The grass is greening. *Spring!*

On the first sixty-degree day, off went people's warm jackets; on came the shorts and sandals. At least that's the way it seemed to me as I made my way to the supermarket. Yards that had been virtually empty all winter were now occupied by people raking leaves, reseeding bare spots, and pruning evergreens. Children ran happily about, unhampered by coats, gloves, caps, and boots. *Spring!*

I thought back to the time of year my husband passed away. Autumn and winter were coming.

"How many seasons," I had asked the Lord, "will I continue to see without my husband here with me?"

There have been eleven springs since then. Although I still whisper, "Honey, I wish you were here," I exult in each change of season. There is a feeling of excitement and expectation.

In spring, there is wonder in the return of life to trees and plants that seemed so barren and colorless. Summer calls for rejoicing in warm days spent out of doors, playing and working. Autumn awes us with its vivid colors, cool evenings, and earlier sunsets that forecast the coming cold days of winter with snow and ice. I look forward to cozy times inside, curled up with books saved for such days.

All through the seasons, God is in control.

God thunders marvelously with His voice;
great things He does which we cannot comprehend.
(Job 37:5)

God is in control of all our seasons.

Prayer

All Your creation praises You, O Lord. I praise You, too, and thank You for senses alert to all You have created and given us to enjoy during our stay on earth. In Jesus' name. Amen.

Learning God's Will

All Scripture is given by inspiration of God, and is profitable for doctrine, for reproof, for correction, for instruction in righteousness. (2 Timothy 3:16)

Some testimonies I have heard in my life have made a lasting impression on me and come to mind at appropriate times. One such testimony I heard in my teens. It was told by a missionary who worked within an African tribe where people were responding eagerly to the gospel. He encouraged them to memorize Scripture. One special young man seemed to memorize a great deal of Scripture. One day, after the young Christian had recited some verses, the missionary asked him, "Do you understand the words you have recited?"

"Oh, yes!" the young man replied earnestly. "First, I practice what the words say until I think I am fully obeying them, then I go on to the next words and do the same."

Would that I always showed such wisdom as I read my Bible!

There is much discussion among Christians about "knowing the will of God." As I was reading from Luke 6 the other morning, I stopped and said to myself, "To obey these words is the will of God."

I had read this chapter many times. I could quote it. Was I fully obeying the words? Recent occurrences in my life convinced me that I was not and that I should be. God did not give me these words to skim over lightly in daily Bible reading or to simply memorize. They were given as His will and *to obey*.

Jesus said, "If you love Me, keep My commandments" (John 14:15).

Another time He said that His words were not burdensome but He had also given us a helper, the Holy Spirit, to enable us to keep them.

To do what God's Word tells us to do—*that is His will*.

Prayer

Father, how many times I stumble and sin because I do not obey Your words. Help me to keep them in my heart and obey them. In Jesus' name. Amen.

Learning at the Cross

*Teach me Your way, O LORD; I will walk
in Your truth; unite my heart to fear Your name.*
(Psalm 86:11)

When I was twenty-one, I was given a book by my mother which I have read many times. It has become a classic, printed in at least seventeen different languages, and has sold millions of copies.

The book is *In His Steps* by Charles Sheldon. It has inspired many people to a closer walk with their Lord. All learn in due time, as I have, that this walk cannot take place without the help of Jesus.

"Without Me," Jesus said, "you can do nothing" (John 15:5).

As I enter into another Easter season, I am reminded that walking in His steps calls for suffering, rejection by others, humility, obedience to God, and genuine love—the love of God which we all need and should desire in our hearts.

As I take the bread and cup at communion, I remember what great anguish Jesus felt as He kneeled in prayer at Gethsemane and asked if the cup of suffering might be taken from Him.

"But not what I will, but what You will be done," He told His Father.

I cannot fully know how terrible it was for Him to take the sins of the whole world upon His sinless, holy body. But He did, and I bow in gratitude for His willingness to die for me, unworthy as I am.

One year our church choir had, for their Easter program, the theme, "I cannot forget the cross." I cannot. I must not. I need to remember this cross throughout the year, not only on Good Friday.

I give thanks for the cross.

Prayer

Help me to walk in Your steps, Lord. It seems easier to go my own way instead of Yours, but Your way is the true way. Thank You for showing us the way and giving us the power to walk in it. In Jesus' name. Amen.

Learning from Déjà Vu

That which has been is what will be, that which is done is what will be done, and there is nothing new under the sun. (Ecclesiastes 1:9)

I love to read to my grandchildren. I always read to our three sons when they were small, too. My oldest grandson, at nine years, had me read Jack London's *Silver Chief* to him during one summer's vacation together. I soon found I did not dare skip over one word and realized my grandson was reading with me. But when I said, "You can read this yourself," he protested. "I want you to read it, Grandma." So I did.

Now my four-year-old grandson brings me his books, and I read to him. When I reach the end of a story he says, "Read it again, Nama."

I told his mother one day I remembered when his daddy, my son, was almost four. My mother-in-law was staying with us, recuperating from surgery. My son brought his books to his grandma where she sat on the couch. Patiently and lovingly she read them, over and over.

So many things we do as parents and grandparents have been done by our parents and grandparents when we were young.

"Is today Tuesday, the twenty-seventh?" one of my children's peers asked me as she wrote out a check.

"All day," I replied.

"That's what my mother always says," she said laughing.

"So did my father," I answered, chuckling, too.

History and people repeat themselves. It would be better if we only repeated the good and not the mistakes. But God knows we do not always learn from our mistakes.

It is good when I remember my parents' faith in God and how God guided them. Then I thank God for His guidance in my life and pray the same will be true for my children and grandchildren.

God never changes.

Prayer

Oh, Thou, who art, who was, and is to come, to You we look for guidance. Your loving-kindness and faithfulness are forever. Thank You in Jesus' name. Amen.

Learning As We Sing

Speaking to one another in psalms and hymns
and spiritual songs, singing and making melody in
your heart to the Lord. (Ephesians 5:19)

The choir anthem ended with a resounding, "Alleluia! Alleluia!" My heart was bursting with praise to God. I had felt the same way when I read one of the psalms of praise in my morning's devotions.

Psalm 92 is called a song for the Sabbath. The psalmist writes, "It is good to give thanks to the LORD, and to sing praises to Your name, O Most High" (Ps. 92:1).

When I was a young girl I sang as I played the piano. I sang at school and church. I didn't know then that I didn't carry a tune very well. I sang the melody the way I thought it sounded, but I could not sing "parts" as accomplished singers could.

So, even though I loved to sing, when I realized I didn't have this talent I did not sing very loudly in a group. I still sing when by myself or rocking my grandchildren. They don't seem to mind that I am not a Barbra Streisand or Lily Pons.

One day, a young man leading our congregational singing at church made this statement: "Too often we sing words without thinking of their meaning. As we sing hymns we should concentrate on the words. Do we mean them? Are we telling God the truth in song? Do we, who would not lie otherwise, sometimes lie as we sing hymns?"

Since that time I've tried to concentrate on the meaning of what I am singing. Do I mean it when I say, "Take my life and let it be consecrated, Lord, to Thee?"

The songs that come from your heart to the Lord can change depression to gladness, despair to hope, and sadness to joy.

So I sing, even if it's only a "joyful noise."

Prayer

Give me a song every day to sing to You, Lord. Let me sing it truthfully. In Jesus' name. Amen.

Learning to Persevere

Then He spoke a parable to them,
that men always ought to pray and not lose heart.
(Luke 18:1)

"Are we almost there? Did you bring my kite?"

The tiny voice persisted until finally his preoccupied mother answered.

"Yes, we're almost there, and I brought your kite."

Seated beside my four-year-old grandson, I couldn't help but admire his determination to get an answer even though I knew his mother was concentrating on other things.

Of course, it can be annoying to have someone continually insist on an answer when we are busy or in a hurry. Perhaps we feel we have already answered. But children, especially, seem determined to receive an answer to their petitions every time they voice them.

Jesus wants us to be like children. He wants us to come to Him, because He has all the answers to our petitions and needs. He told His disciples, "Keep asking, keep seeking, and keep knocking, because you will receive an answer."

Sometimes the answer isn't the one we desire. When a parent gives answers such as "wait," "no," or "we're going to have something better," children fuss and are not satisfied. They want what they ask for, and they want it now.

Oh, how many times I have responded like a fussy, unhappy child. I understand my Father in heaven knows what is best for me, but I'd really like Him to answer according to my desires and *immediately*.

God is greater, wiser, more loving than I deserve.

Prayer

You say, "Wait," "No," or "I have something better for you," and I am not always happy with Your answer to my prayers, Father. Forgive me and help me to trust Your answers and obey Your Word. In Jesus' name. Amen.

Learning to Run

Let us lay aside every weight, and the sin which so easily ensnares us, and let us run with endurance the race that is set before us. (Hebrews 12:1)

I am not much of a runner. I'd rather walk than jog. Of course, I ran when I was younger. I did not have any physical problems to slow me down or keep me from running then. I enjoy watching others run now, but I am content to walk myself.

However, there is a race I must run. It is the race that we run as Christians, with our eyes on Jesus, the author and finisher of our faith. The Bible says we are surrounded by witnesses who have already run the race and shown us how to do it.

I've watched people running competitive races. They dress lightly and do not carry any unnecessary weight. They keep their eyes on the goal and exert all their energy to reach it. I heard one runner say, "I looked back, and it made me slow down."

The apostle Paul must have known all about foot races. He knew that keeping our eyes on the goal and not letting anything hinder us was important. In our Christian walk, it is sin that causes us to stumble and lag behind. We can become discouraged if we look back at our past sins and dwell on them. If we've confessed them and repented of them we are forgiven. We can't run well if we're "looking back."

Hebrews 12 gives examples of those who have gone ahead of us. I can think of people I have known who trusted and followed Jesus. They showed me the way and encouraged me as I began my new life in Christ.

Our Christian race has an eternal goal.

Prayer

I thank You, Father, for the patience and faith You have given me to run the race You have set before me. In Jesus' name. Amen.

Learning While Losing Things

*"What woman, having ten silver coins, if she
loses one coin, does not light a lamp, sweep
the house, and seek diligently until she finds it?"*
(Luke 15:8)

I lose things easily.

I felt an instant kinship with a woman speaker I once heard who said, "I think I've lost more things than I've ever owned."

Losing my handbag at a small restaurant the day before seemed to top my list of "losing things." I called, and the manager looked in the safe and said that he found only one handbag there, and it had been in the safe a week. Well, so someone else loses things. It was no consolation.

A friend who had been with me at the restaurant said I should cancel my credit cards right away. But this was Sunday. I decided to call the restaurant again and ask if I should report my loss to the police. The manager looked again. My handbag was there. A waiter had put it under the counter instead of the safe when it was turned in.

I thanked the Lord all the way to the restaurant to pick it up and then all the way to church.

Another friend said, "Isn't God good!"

Indeed He is. He came to seek and save those who were lost.

My grandson and I love to read a child's book about the Good Shepherd and how the Shepherd cares for His sheep and lambs. One lamb is lost. It is dark, and the lamb is afraid. The Shepherd hears its cries, finds it, and takes it back to the fold. Happy ending!

I was happy when I found my handbag. How much greater the joy in heaven, Jesus says, over one sinner who repents, over who was lost and is found.

It's good news when the lost are found!

Prayer

Help me, Lord, to be more careful. Thank You that, though I was lost, You found me and gave me the gift of eternal life in Jesus Christ, our Lord. Amen.

Learning from a Cheerful Person

A merry heart does good, like medicine.
(Proverbs 17:22)

As I stood in line at the post office waiting my turn to be helped, I watched one postal clerk. I couldn't ever remember seeing her without a smile. She greeted each customer cheerfully and her smile stayed as she chatted, listened, and helped them. I learned it was her last day at the branch as she was being transferred to another.

"We'll miss your cheerful smile and helpfulness," I told her.

"Thank you," she said, and her smile grew even brighter. "Those nice words deserve something." And she handed me a candy kiss from the sack near her.

I thanked her and said, "I know you'll be a welcome help wherever you're going."

Serving the public, I know from past experience, isn't always easy. Some customers complain or are angry. Some are easily upset. The way people are served can make a difference in their response. It's hard to stay angry with someone who smiles at you and tries to be helpful.

Jesus is our example of the perfect servant. He never returned evil for evil. He was God, but He humbled Himself to become a man and endure the same things we do. People treated Him badly. He was wrongly accused. He was mistrusted. He was sometimes too busy to eat or rest. He saw and met the needs of those who came to Him. He loved the world and that was evident in His life, death, and resurrection. All for us.

Simply thinking of Jesus' love makes me smile.

Prayer

Help me to serve You and others cheerfully.
In Jesus' name. Amen.

Learning Inward Renewal

Even though our outward man is perishing,
yet the inward man is being renewed day by day.
(2 Corinthians 4:16)

I used to wonder why my parents, aunts, uncles, and other older people enjoyed reminiscing about earlier days. I wonder no longer. I find myself saying "remember when" more often nowadays.

My father used to say he could remember things that happened many years ago but couldn't always remember what he did an hour ago. I laughed when he said that. I don't laugh now, as I search for something I put down somewhere a little while ago.

I notice more of my peers discussing physical ailments, medicine, and doctors. I listen sympathetically and think about the bunion I should have removed.

A friend of mine smiles at these things and quotes from Paul's letter to the Corinthians. It says, "these are momentary light afflictions."

And that's right. In the light of eternity, our temporal problems do not have the same importance. Learning to trust God with everything and live each day trying to learn what is pleasing to Him, gives a different perspective to our life here on earth.

More wrinkles, graying hair, bifocals, trifocals, hearing aids! All these are outward manifestations of aging. I give them my concern and attention when necessary, but I've learned not to focus my thoughts on them. I've also learned that what I see in other people and what they see in me is primarily the inner person that reflects who we really are.

Growing older is part of life.

Prayer

Thank You for the days allotted me. Help me to live them thankfully, prayerfully, and in a way that is pleasing to You. In Jesus' name. Amen.

Learning During Special Moments

But Mary kept all these things and pondered
them in her heart. (Luke 2:19)

I had never known a Christmas Day quite like this one. Here I was, hiking in the snowy woods with my middle son and six-foot-six-inch grandson. The air was crisp and still—thirty degrees and no wind. Below us a tiny creek flowed, sometimes under the ice and sometimes breaking through for a long stretch. A rabbit darted out from brush a few feet from me. I smiled, watching his white tail disappear as he sought a safer hiding place. Cock and hen pheasants flew up with whirring wings as we crossed a weedy field. Back in the woods, we saw tiny gray birds flitting from branch to branch on low bushes. High in a tree, my menfolk spotted an owl who watched us, too.

We hoped to see deer so we went by way of separate trails, thinking one of us would find a few for all to see. My grandson spotted three, but my son and I didn't hear him calling so we missed seeing them. I wasn't overly disappointed. The two-hour hike had been invigorating and uplifting, and I thanked God for the beauty of His creation around us. I also thanked Him for my two husky companions.

My son was visiting from Alaska and my grandson from his air force base in Texas. In a week, they would be returning home. These were special moments for me.

At Christmastime each year, we hear again and again the wonderful story of our Savior's miraculous birth. The Creator became a baby to fulfill His plan for our salvation.

That was a *very* special moment.

Prayer

*Thank You, Lord, for daily life, filled with moments
to be appreciated. Help me to savor them and not be hurrying
on to other things. In Jesus' name. Amen.*

Learning to Work Together

*From whom the whole body, joined and knit together
by what every joint supplies, according to the effective
working by which every part does its share, causes
growth of the body for the edifying of itself in love.*
(Ephesians 4:16)

Every spring, summer, and fall the entrance to my
church is made beautiful by many bright-colored flowers
that line the entranceway from the street to the doors of
the church. People gasp and exclaim in admiration as they
walk or drive by them.

This beautiful array is the work of many. Some prepare
the ground for planting; others choose and buy the plants,
plant them, water and fertilize them. All during the season,
willing workers weed, water, and take care of the flowers.

This may seem, to some, a small way to serve God in the church. And there are other tasks that may seem minor, but each serves a necessary purpose. If even one were neglected, there would soon be a realization that something was missing in the work of the church.

The other evening I made waffles for my son and family. They tasted all right but we all felt they weren't quite as good as usual.

When I began moving dishes to the cupboard I saw the bowl of egg whites I had intended to add to my batter. A minor ingredient? Well, perhaps, but they were what was lacking in the waffles.

The tiniest bolt can make a difference if it is missing from an engine. Missing stitches can cause a garment to fall apart. And a missing ingredient can spoil a recipe. So each member of God's church is important.

For in fact the body is not one member but many.
(1 Corinthians 12:14)

Prayer

Help me to do cheerfully and willingly whatever You
have for me to do, Lord, whether it's a small or large task.
In Jesus' name. Amen.

Learning to Receive

*Every good gift and every perfect gift is from above,
and comes down from the Father of lights, with whom
there is no variation or shadow of turning.*
(James 1:17)

There must be receivers when there are givers. And receiving a gift well is, in itself, a measure of giving.

"Here, Nama, is a 'bokay' for you."

My four-and-a-half-year-old grandson handed me the purple flowers he had clutched in his tiny hands.

"Thank you, Aaron. They are beautiful," I said.

Weeds they might be to others, but not to a grandmother—or mother.

Aaron watched in delight as I arranged them carefully in a glass of water and set them on the table. Grandma liked his gift.

Too often I have spoiled someone else's gift to me by immediately giving them a gift in return. I have insisted in paying someone for a job they had done in love and concern. I have spoiled someone's giving by saying, "Oh, now what can I give you?"

When a young man came unexpectedly and mowed my lawn, I pressed a ten-dollar bill in his hand.

I could tell immediately I had hurt him by paying him. He had wanted to help me with what was actually a big job. He offered to mow again but insisted he didn't want to be paid.

"When are you going to learn to receive as well as give?" my father used to rebuke me, when I was ungracious in receiving.

Jesus took five barley loaves and two fishes from a little boy and gave thanks for them (John 6:9–11).

Prayer

You gave Your Son to die in my place, Father. Nothing I could give You in return would be enough. So when I say, Lord, take my life and use it, it is because I took Your gift, thankfully. In Jesus' name. Amen.

Learning God's Voice

"And when he brings out his own sheep,
he goes before them; and the sheep follow him,
for they know his voice." (John 10:4)

"Mommy! Mommy!"

The terrified voice of the child rose from the long aisles of the store.

"I'll help you find her." "Don't cry. Come here." People spoke comfortingly to the child but the little lad didn't seem to hear them.

"Michael, Michael!"

That was the right voice, and the boy ran to the sound of it. Soon he was in his mother's arms.

A mother can usually pick out her child's voice from a group, especially if the child is in distress. And the child recognizes his mother's comforting voice over all others.

How welcome the sound of a familiar voice is to the one who is lost.

We are studying the gospel of John in our adult Sunday school class. Last Sunday our teacher said, "When I was a child, I would visit my grandparents' farm. When the cows came to the barn at milking time, Grandma would say, 'Don't stand by the gate; they don't know you and won't come in.' She was right. They only came in at my grandparents' presence or voice."

God speaks to His children through His Word. The more we study the Bible, the more we come to recognize His voice. When we hear teaching that is strange and different from what He has told us, we should not follow it. We should turn to His familiar voice for direction and hear Him say, "I am the way, the truth, and the life" (John 14:6).

Children know their mother's voice.

Children of God know their Father's voice.

Prayer

Help me always to follow Your voice, Father. Let me not be deceived by the voice of strangers. In Christ's name. Amen.

Learning About Possessions

And He said to them, "Take heed and beware of covetousness, for one's life does not consist in the abundance of the things he possesses. . . . For where your treasure is, there will your heart be also."
(Luke 12:15, 34)

In bold black letters the headlines of the morning paper told of another fire. It had destroyed the entire building and all that was in it. Thankfully, there were no people in it.

That was the sixth or seventh fire our city had experienced in the last two weeks of January. To add to the fire department's problems, we in the Midwest were experiencing, what one newsman had labeled, "a deep freeze."

One of the fires had been in a school. It had been reported quickly, so teachers and students were able to carry out important papers, books, and some furniture before the fire spread.

"What would you do if your house were on fire?" I asked myself. "Would you be able to save any of your possessions?"

There is so much I'd hate to lose. Pictures, a grandfather clock my husband had built from a kit, a rug he latch-hooked —oh, so many things with special memories, things that could not be replaced.

I stopped. What had Jesus said? "Our life does not consist in our possessions." Yes, they have special meaning because they all remind me of those I love. But they are not to take first place in my life. If I were to lose them all, but was rich in God, I would still have treasure in heaven, which is much more important.

Possessions should not possess me.

Prayer

Keep me putting things in the right perspective, Father.
All that I have is from Your hand, but things that are eternal
are the most important. In Jesus' name. Amen.

Learning About Heaven

Beloved, now we are children of God; and it has not
yet been revealed what we shall be, but we know that
when He is revealed, we shall be like Him, for we
shall see Him as He is. (1 John 3:2)

"I'm looking forward to heaven. Then I'll be able to walk without crutches, and I'll have a new body."

I looked at her forty-year-old body, crippled from birth, and thought how I didn't really see her disability now that I've come to know her better. I see God's love shining in her eyes, in her words, and in her actions.

"Just think. The first face I'll see when I can see again is the face of Jesus," the young man said.

Born a diabetic, he had been blind now for several years. As he approached his forties, and his love for his Savior grew, his thoughts often went to heaven.

I've found my thoughts on heaven more since the passing away of my husband, father, mother, and other relatives and friends.

"What will it be like? What will we do there? Will we be with those we've known on earth?"

I realize, as Deuteronomy 29:29 says, "the secret things belong to the LORD our God," but God has revealed glimpses in His Word about heaven.

We know that the angels, God's messengers, live there and serve God and us, His children: "For He shall give His angels charge over you, to keep you in all your ways" (Ps. 91:11).

The Bible says that, in the new heaven, "God will wipe away every tear from their eyes; there shall be no more death, nor sorrow, nor crying; and there shall be no more pain" (Rev. 21:4).

And we shall be with the Lord forever!

Prayer

I'm looking forward to heaven, too, Father, knowing that wherever You are is where I want to be. In Christ. Amen.

Learning
As Life Lengthens

When I awake, I am still with You.
(Psalm 139:18)

"I wake up in the morning and say, 'Well, I'm still here.'"
The ninety-nine-year-old's eyes crinkled in laughter as she talked to my sister and me.

We laughed, too. The tiny lady was so cheerful and full of life. We were enjoying our time with her immensely.

"Oh, you look wonderful," she exclaimed when we walked into her room. "So young and lovely."

Oh, yes, we loved that. Not too many people say that to you when you are over sixty.

Her smile never faded as we listened and talked with her. Although her hearing was poor, she did not let that keep her from enjoying our visit. We learned she could still read the daily paper and watch television. She helped her daughter fold clothes and demanded little attention for herself. How wonderful, we thought, to be ninety-nine and still enjoy life. We knew she had still grown a vegetable garden when she was ninety.

"But I'm prepared," she said. "I'm prepared for my time to leave this earth."

"I am, too," I said.

"Good! Good!" she said, clapping her hands.

Nothing brings more joy than knowing you are prepared to meet God because you have trusted His Son for your salvation. Knowing that He died for your sins and having accepted His free gift, you can say when your life on this earth is over, "I am still with You."

Prayer

Thank You, Father, for Your nearness. Whether my days be few or many, You remain the same. What a blessed assurance. In Jesus' name. Amen.

Learning
How to Think

Finally, brethren, whatever things are true,
whatever things are noble, whatever things
are just, whatever things are pure, . . . meditate
on these things. (Philippians 4:8)

"I don't think of what I can't eat. I think of what I can," my friend said, smiling cheerfully.

She had been telling me about the new diet her doctor had given her to help her with physical problems she had been having.

"You have a good attitude toward your diet," I said.

"It sure makes it a lot easier to follow," she laughed. And, of course, she was right.

What we think usually ends up coming out in our words and actions. If we think angry thoughts, angry words follow. Self-pitying thoughts produce complaining words.

When I go about my daily work singing hymns, it affects my attitude, and I am more likely to answer someone cheerfully.

When I spilled a glass of orange juice over my recently scrubbed floor I remembered my friend's words and didn't dwell on what had happened. As I wiped the floor clean again I thought, "Well, it wasn't sticky waffle syrup I spilled. I can wipe this juice up easily." And I did.

My last visit to the doctor resulted in orders not to eat chocolate, peppermint, or drink carbonated drinks.

"Chocolate," I groaned. Then I asked, "How about popcorn?"

"You can eat popcorn," he said, smiling.

And I smiled, too. Although I love chocolate, it would not be missed as much if I could still eat popcorn. This must be partly what Paul meant when he said to be content in whatever circumstances we find ourselves. Thinking about what we have, instead of what we don't have, helps us to be content.

Prayer

Thank You, God, for each day's blessings. Help me, Father, to watch my thoughts, that they may be pleasing to You. In Jesus' name. Amen.

Learning from Birthdays

So teach us to number our days, that we may
gain a heart of wisdom. (Psalm 90:12)

Today was my sixty-ninth birthday. Family and friends remembered me with cards and gifts. I was the special guest at a family dinner. As the day came to a pleasant close and I was back in my own home, alone, I remembered other birthdays.

Certain ones stand out! A surprise party my mother gave me when I was sixteen. A gag gift on my twenty-first birthday from Jim, instead of an engagement ring. All because I thought it would be romantic to become engaged on Valentine's Day a month later. And it was. I remembered gifts from young sons doing their first shopping. A figurine of an old-fashioned girl and her dog, a twelve-sided wooden paperweight with inspirational sayings on each side, and once, an egg slicer. All were special to me. I cherished cards given by my husband with messages not easily spoken by this quiet man. Saved now and reread. There were humorous cards from grown sons and from my brother. And there are other special cards in my memory box; cards from my sister, from a grandmother now gone, a card from a lady who taught me a great deal about writing. She'd sent it when she was past ninety. I suppose some day someone will have to discard my treasured cards. I can't.

This birthday held a sad note. This time the two who brought me into this world were not a part of it. Both gone—Dad over two years ago and Mother almost a year. I had been blessed with having them for so many years, but I miss being a daughter.

Although life on earth is full of changes, it is reassuring to know that Jesus never changes. He is the same, "Yesterday, today, and forever" (Heb. 13:8). As my Savior and Lord, He is my rock on whom I can always depend.

Prayer

Thank You, Lord, for Your steadfastness and faithfulness.
In Jesus' name. Amen.

Learning to Seek

And you will seek Me and find Me, when you search
for Me with all your heart. (Jeremiah 29:13)

Playing hide-and-seek with a three-year-old is an experience. But children love to play it. My grandson, Austin,
hides in the same place every time.

We were playing hide-and-seek in the house on a rainy
day. When it was my turn to hide, Austin would count his
imitation of my count, "One, two, three, six, nine, eight,
thirteen, twenty. Ready or not, here I come." Then he would
rush down the hallway saying, "Grandma, where are you?"
To help him, I would make a little sound. When he still
could not find me, his call would become a little more plain-
tive. I'd make a louder sound and, when he finally found
me, his laughter was both joyous and relieved. When I encouraged him to hide in a different place, as I did, he would

tell me where he was going to hide. To him, hide-and-seek meant finding or being found right away.

God doesn't play hide-and-seek with us, but there are times when our sins separate us from God, as it says in Isaiah 59:2. But "if we confess our sins, He is faithful and just to forgive us our sins and to cleanse us from all unrighteousness" (1 John 1:9).

> *The Lord is near to all who call upon Him, to all who call upon Him in truth. (Psalm 145:18)*

God tells us how we can find Him and, when we respond to His voice, we find Him and are happy. He wants us to find Him. He is always the same, and He is more ready to answer than we are to call.

Jesus said, "Seek, and you will find" (Matt. 7:7).

Prayer

Thank You, Lord, for Your precious promises given in love. You want us to find You. Forgive my sins and hear my prayer. In Jesus' name. Amen.

Learning Joy Anew

*My brethren, count it all joy when you fall
into various trials. (James 1:2)*

All through the night it snowed! I could hear loud thuds, and one especially loud one, on the roof above me. But it wasn't until the morning light that I could see the devastation outside. Tree branches from my two forty-two-year-old pin oaks covered my lawn, driveway, and sidewalk. The large thud on my roof was explained when I saw a huge limb from the old elm tree in back lying partly on the roof. As I listened to the radio, I heard of this same destruction covering our entire city and nearby areas. All over the state, roads were blocked and travelers were stranded. Airports were not operating. The mayor came on the air to assure the citizens that all was being done that could possibly be done to clear streets and restore electric power.

I hadn't lost power and was thankful for that. The sight of the destruction outside had been overwhelming, but I could be thankful for much: warmth, safety, and loving children who checked on me and would help me as soon as they could.

The verse impressed on the class by the teacher of our home Bible study the past few weeks flashed through my mind. "Count it all joy," he had said. Another version of the Bible added the words, "when you encounter various trials."

While the scene before me wasn't one to naturally inspire joy, the following verse in James reads, "The testing of your faith produces patience" (1:3).

Yes, we can have joy in trials knowing that God is with us in all of them and, through them, is working out His purpose in our lives.

Prayer

*God of all comfort, who gives us daily what is necessary
and teaches us to trust during trials and temptations,
I thank You and consider it joy to have You as my teacher.
In Jesus' name. Amen.*

Learning All Through Life

But grow in the grace and knowledge of our Lord and Savior Jesus Christ. To Him be the glory both now and forever. Amen. (2 Peter 3:18)

"You'll learn soon enough." These words can be an encouragement or a warning, depending on how they are used. Either way, they can impart more knowledge.

We learn to acquire new skills by perseverance. We learn that doing dangerous things or disobeying authority brings harm or correction.

Training children in all the things they need to know takes time. Using "please" and "thank you," toilet training, tying shoelaces, looking when crossing the street—the list goes on and on.

As the years roll by, I am learning that the words spoken by an older friend are true.

"Learning takes a lifetime," she said.

How wise her words! How encouraging!

Sometimes the very hardest things to learn are the things relating to our spiritual growth.

"Will I ever learn to be slow to speak?" I mourned as I realized I had just spoken too hastily—again!

I have memorized Scripture verses that help, and I try to repeat them each day. Memorizing the entire book of James has brought many "tongue" admonitions to my mind exactly when I needed them.

Learning may be slow and difficult for some, due to physical disabilities or health problems. But God gives patience and understanding to those who teach disabled learners.

Perhaps the time will come when I am forgetful or unable to think for myself. We do not know what tomorrow will bring. Now is the time to learn from His Word so we may grow spiritually every day.

Prayer

Thank You, God, for the ability You have given us to learn. You are a patient and loving teacher. Keep me ever learning until my life on earth ends. In Jesus' name. Amen.

Learning As God Teaches

*In all your ways acknowledge Him, and He shall
direct your paths. (Proverbs 3:6)*

"How long have you been widowed?" my new friend asked. "Fifteen years this July," I answered, anticipating her look of amazement.

"Have you ever considered being married again?" she asked hesitantly.

"Yes," I said, "but as I prayed about it, I soon understood this was not God's will for me. So I prayed for contentment."

When I became a widow, I began to be more aware of the way other widows and widowers were relating to their new position in society. It was truly a learning experience. Some women I knew had been widowed for many years, even while they still had children at home. Though they hadn't as yet remarried, they enjoyed the occasional companionship of a man. Some had remarried and were making the necessary adjustments that come with a second marriage. Others had found comfort in joining groups of widows and widowers. All were still individuals with their own personalities. Regardless of similarities in experiences, we are still directed by our own inner feelings that make us who we are.

Proverbs 3:6 became my guide. God directs; I follow. God teaches; I learn.

Prayer

Father, as You direct me, help me to follow, knowing that You know what is best for me always. As You teach, may I learn. In Jesus' name. Amen.